JOHN B. CARROLL

Roy E. Larsen Professor of Educational
Psychology, Graduate School of Education,
Harvard University; author of books and
numerous articles on the psychology and the
teaching of language, and of the Modern
Language Aptitude Test; consulting editor
of several scholarly journals in the fields
of language and educational psychology.

Language
and Thought

PRENTICE-HALL, INC., *Englewood Cliffs, New Jersey*

LANGUAGE AND THOUGHT, *John B. Carroll*

PRENTICE-HALL FOUNDATIONS
OF MODERN PSYCHOLOGY SERIES
Richard S. Lazarus, *Editor*

PRENTICE-HALL INTERNATIONAL, INC., *London*
PRENTICE-HALL OF AUSTRALIA, PTY., LTD., *Sydney*
PRENTICE-HALL OF CANADA, LTD., *Toronto*
PRENTICE-HALL OF INDIA PRIVATE LIMITED, *New Delhi*
PRENTICE-HALL OF JAPAN, INC., *Tokyo*
PRENTICE-HALL DE MEXICO, S.A., *Mexico City*

Designed by Harry Rinehart

C–52270(p), C–52271(c)

Foundations
of Modern Psychology
Series

The tremendous growth and vitality of psychology and its increasing fusion with the social and biological sciences demand a new approach to teaching at the introductory level. The basic course, geared as it usually is to a single text that tries to skim everything—that sacrifices depth for superficial breadth—is no longer adequate. Psychology has become too diverse for any one man, or a few men, to write about with complete authority. The alternative, a book that ignores many essential areas in order to present more comprehensively and effectively a particular aspect or view of psychology, is also insufficient. For in this solution, many key areas are simply not communicated to the student at all.

The Foundations of Modern Psychology is a new and different approach to the introductory course. The instructor is offered a series of short volumes, each a self-contained book on the special issues, methods, and content of a basic topic by a noted authority who is actively contributing to that particular field. And taken together, the volumes cover the full scope of psychological thought, research, and application.

The result is a series that offers the advantage of tremendous flexibility and scope. The teacher can choose the subjects he wants to emphasize and present them in the order he desires. And without necessarily sacrificing breadth, he can provide the student with a much fuller treatment of individual areas at the introductory level than is normally possible. If he does not have time to include all the volumes in his course, he can recommend the omitted ones as outside reading, thus covering the full range of psychological topics.

Psychologists are becoming increasingly aware of the importance of reaching the introductory student with high-quality, well-written, and stimulating material, material that highlights the continuing and exciting search for new knowledge. The Foundations of Modern Psychology Series is our attempt to place in the hands of instructors the best textbook tools for this purpose.

Preface

In writing this book on the psychology of language and thought I have tried to make it come as close as possible to my ideal of what a presentation of this topic should be in an introductory course in psychology. In my use of scientific linguistics as a foundation and point of departure, I have produced a treatment that I believe you would find somewhat different from those in typical texts. I have been quite deliberate about this, however, because I believe that the psychological study of language and thought requires first an accurate knowledge of what language is.

Thus, more is said about language than about thought. But this is more a reflection of the advanced state of our knowledge about language and the primitive state of our knowledge about thought than of my true opinion about the relative importance of the topics. We need very much to know more about thinking than we do. One of the major themes of this book is that thought and cognition are presupposed by language—that speech is a consequence of some kind of thought or cognition, even though language structure may channel or influence thought.

The psychology of language and thought has only recently become a well-respected and eagerly pursued field of research. I have attempted to describe a sample of the more useful and interesting results obtained thus far, along with an account of the theoretical developments that underlie them. I feel certain that the psychology of language and thought as a body of knowledge already has important implications for psychology in general, for particular problems in education, and for everyday life. But at many points I have had to indulge in speculation, going beyond the sure data we have. Frequently I have had to characterize statements or ideas as being only "probable" or "approximate" or even just "possible." I hope that in so doing I may arouse your interest, in the wish that some day a more objective account of the psychology of language and thought, better grounded in observation and experiment, can be written.

John B. Carroll

Contents

Contents

Contents

x

Language
and Communication

"Speech," wrote Benjamin Lee Whorf,[1] "is the best show man puts on." It is the task of this book to elucidate the full meaning of this statement, by describing exactly what this "show" consists of, and by attempting to explain how man is able to "put on" such a marvelous display. More than that, we shall try to say how this capacity helps man in his thinking, and suggest how it can sometimes work against his best interests. We shall discuss how individuals acquire language skills, how they differ in their facility in language, and how speech functions are disturbed in aphasia, the psychoses,

[1] B. L. Whorf. *Language, thought and reality.* Cambridge and New York: M.I.T.-Wiley, 1956, p. 249.

I

and other disorders. All this knowledge, it is hoped, will aid you in understanding the role of language and thought in your own and others' behavior and supply a necessary background for applications of the psychology of language in other branches of psychology, in education, and elsewhere.

In sheer volume, speech behavior can yield impressive statistics. It may be an interesting exercise for you to measure the average rate (words per minute) at which you speak in spontaneous conversation, and then to estimate the probable number of words you speak in a day, a month, or a year. A person would not have to be a particularly talkative individual to speak a billion words in a lifetime. A professional writer who averages 2000 written words as his daily output would turn out 730,000 words a year; it has been reckoned that the German psychologist Wilhelm Wundt published 53,735 printed pages in the 68 years of his career, or about one word every two minutes, night and day.

On the input side, the intake of speech or writing by the average individual is tremendous. A student attending classes and holding frequent conversations with fellow-students might hear 100,000 words in a day. If he has a modest reading speed of, say, 300 words per minute and spends five hours a day reading, he would cover 90,000 words a day. Such a student, then, could easily be exposed to three-quarters of a billion words a year.

Not all these words would be different, of course; indeed, it is likely that about one in ten is the word *the*. Notice the distinction between a word as a *type* and a word as a *token*: *The* simply as a word is a type, whereas each instance of it in use is a token. In telephone conversation, 50 common word types make up about 60 per cent of all the word tokens. Nevertheless, the number of types found can be very large, if large enough samples are taken. Even though an individual may not use certain words more than once in a very long time, if he is highly educated he may have a vocabulary of well over 100,000 different words, particularly if one includes all the proper names of people and places that he knows. Because of certain methodological difficulties, research has not yet given clear answers on the magnitude of individual vocabularies, but we can confidently say that word types constitute the largest single set of different learned responses of human beings.

But speech behavior cannot be measured solely in words. The sounds that compose the words, the inflections of the voice, and the ways the words are composed and arranged are all essential elements of speech. In addition, a talker is most likely to accompany his speech with gestures and facial expressions that add emphasis or nuance. Of even more importance to a psychologist, the behavior of the talker represents some kind of message, and behind this message one is tempted to infer the operation of a host of psychological processes commonly identified under such names as perceiving, desiring, willing, thinking, believing, and feeling. Around 1900, a favorite method of psychology was to ask subjects to "introspect," that is, to make careful verbal reports on their own mental processes. Nowadays, less confidence is placed in such subjective reports, but it remains true that what a person says or writes constitutes overt behavior that is potentially grist for the psychologist's mill if he will take the trouble to study it objectively and with due regard for other kinds of information about behavior.

It will be well to define our terms. *Speech behavior* is that overt activity in which the muscles controlling the diaphragm, the larynx, and the various parts of the mouth are used to produce *utterances* exhibiting regularities that depend on a system of vocal communication we call *language*. In order for a language to exist, there must be a *speech community,* that is, a group of individuals who are able to communicate with one another because they have learned to respond to one another's utterances in consistent ways. In certain psychological experiments, the experimenter and the subject in effect constitute a miniature speech community; the experimenter arranges matters, say, so that the subject gets rewarded only if he learns to say "zik" when he sees "MUQ," or the experimenter plays a game with the subject in which the latter must discover what classes of stimuli are to be called "zugs." *Natural* languages like English, Chinese, or Navaho have speech communities composed of thousands or even millions of speakers who have all learned a large number of responses in common. Furthermore, the regularities found in the language systems used by these speech communities are both numerous and complex.

In theory, a language can be a system underlying any set of responses of which human beings are capable; thus, it is not entirely inappropriate, in some contexts, to speak of "the language of mathematics" or "the language of flowers." However, for our present purposes, we shall use it only for the sort of system that underlies the oral communication of a speech community. Occasionally it may be useful to extend the concept of language to include the system of gestures and facial expressions that ordinarily accompany speech behavior, but this system is largely dependent on speech behavior and does not exhibit the degree of complexity shown by the spoken language system. It is beyond the scope of the present treatment to discuss the possible "linguistic" status of still other systems of behavior that may play a part in communication, like the "expressive movements" exhibited in various performances such as handwriting that G. W. Allport and P. Vernon have studied,[2] the styles of culturally conditioned behavior called the "silent language" by the anthropologist Edward T. Hall,[3] or the language of visual symbols described by Ruesch and Kees.[4]

Writing, however, is a system of communication that has a special relationship to spoken language in that it depends largely on the prior existence of spoken language. Phylogenetically, man learned to talk before he learned to write, and ontogenetically, the child learns to talk before he learns to write. For this reason, written language must always be regarded as spoken language "written down" in a particular conventionalized writing system and phrased, often, in a special written style. Studying the structure of a language solely in its written form, although useful for some purposes, has its limitations; for example, this method totally ignores the sound system of the language and its possible effects on the structure. In psychological research and experimentation, it can be misleading to use written or printed words as

[2] G. W. Allport and P. E. Vernon. *Studies in expressive movement.* New York: Macmillan, 1933.

[3] E. T. Hall. *The silent language.* New York: Doubleday, 1959.

[4] J. Ruesch and W. Kees. *Nonverbal communication.* Berkeley: University of California Press, 1956.

stimuli without taking proper consideration of the way in which subjects may respond to these stimuli in terms of spoken language. To give a simple illustration, a homograph like LEAD can be highly ambiguous.

There is a cartoon depicting two prehistoric men wondering, now that they had learned to talk, what they would talk about; the humor of it lies mostly in the fact that language would probably never have developed unless it had served some function. We can think of language as serving two major functions: (1) as a system of responses by which individuals communicate with each other (inter-individual communication); and (2) as a system of responses that facilitates thinking and action for the individual (intra-individual communication).

It seems almost too obvious to say that language functions in interpersonal communication—in conveying information, thoughts, and feelings from one person to another and in providing a means by which people control each other's behavior. Such a statement, however, is couched in everyday parlance and is actually difficult to translate into the terms of a purely objective, scientific account of interpersonal behavior. For example, it leaves such terms as "information," "thought," and "feeling" undefined, and fails to explain how anything as apparently insubstantial as language can control behavior. It is no wonder that philosophers and psychologists have had difficulty in clarifying their concepts of the function of language. We shall take the point of view that an objective account of the role of language in communication can be achieved only through an analysis of people's behavior as they use or learn to use language; such an analysis will be attempted in Chapter 3.

Once an individual has learned even a small portion of the responses involved in language, he can start to use them in *intrapersonal* communication, that is, in "thinking" and in the facilitation of his own behavior. For one thing, the individual can respond to his own speech behavior, either with more speech behavior, or with action; he can, for example, respond to verbal representations of previous experience, long after the original experience, and he can give himself commands to act. Furthermore, many language responses come to correspond to what we ordinarily call "concepts." Indeed, they function as names of concepts and therefore can be used as stimuli for evoking and manipulating concepts. This function may be illustrated by the behavior of a person performing an exercise in mental arithmetic. The words he uses in performing this task (for example, "3 times 9 is 27; 7 times 9 is 63, carry 2, so 73 times 9 is 657") stand for concepts (numbers and operations with numbers) that he can manipulate as verbal forms far more easily than as concrete things he might have to count or put together manually. The decimal number system provides a well-organized set of verbal concepts and operations by means of which an individual can communicate with himself (and others). It is far better designed for *human* use than the binary system (that uses only the digits 0 and 1), however appropriate the latter may be for electronic computing machines.

Most systems of concepts are nonnumerical, of course, but the same principle holds. The evidence suggests that, in general, people can "think" better when they have a good stock of well-learned concepts and their names.

Because of the intimate connection between language and conceptualization, we will devote considerable attention, in Chapters 6 and 7, to the nature of concepts, how concepts are learned, and what role they play in behavior.

COMMUNICATION SYSTEMS

In order to study language, it is necessary to gain some perspective on the relation between language and what is called communication. *Communication* is a concept whose scope of application is rather flexible. In the most general sense, communication occurs when some kind of energy is transferred from one place to another, for example when a disturbance occurring on one side of a pond is "communicated" to the other side by a series of waves, or when the energy applied to a sense organ is "communicated" to the brain over a nerve. One might also argue that the appearance of smoke somewhere in the distance "communicates" to an observer that a fire is burning. It could be said that the smoke is a "sign" of fire. Our experience constantly furnishes examples of events or stimuli that are in some way "evidences" or "signs" of various states of affairs, purely through the operation of various physical, chemical, or biological effects, but we do not ordinarily think of such "signs" as constituting elements in a "sign system" like language nor even as messages in a "communication system." A cough may be the sign of a cold, but it is not ordinarily perceived as a contrived, artificial symbol analogous to a word.

We are, after all, interested in a particular kind of communication: communication between persons (or, sometimes, within a person). The communication system that enables human beings to communicate has two major aspects: (1) a physical and biological system in which the communication takes place, and (2) a sign system in which messages are formulated.

If we examine the total system in which communication takes place, we observe that the number of links over which messages may travel in passing from one person's nervous system to another's may be very large. A separate branch of engineering has developed around the problems of making sure that messages flow over the purely physical links (air, telephone wires, microphones, and so on) with minimum error and expense. Various biological and psychological specialists are concerned with the characteristics and capabilities of the biophysical links in the system—the nerves, the speech apparatus, and the auditory receptors (if we consider only the transmission of oral language).

Of much more relevance to psychology, however, is the study of sign systems. Let us examine the sign system of one of the simplest communication arrangements we can think of—that whereby a thermostat controls the operation of a heating plant. Here we observe the three essential properties of all sign systems, namely:

1. *A finite set of discrete signs.* In this case there are only two signs: the flow of an electric current, or the absence of such a current. The thermostat,

which originates messages, is able to produce both these signs in such a way that they are readily discriminable by the sensing mechanism (probably an electric relay), which turns the heating plant on or off.

2. *Referential function of the signs.* Each of the two signs in the system represents or reflects a different state of objective reality—(a) a temperature as high as, or higher than, a given setting, or (b) a temperature lower than the given setting. These signs are generated by the mechanism of the thermostat.

3. *Arbitrariness of the sign system.* Deciding which sign is to represent which state is (at least in principle) arbitrary; it depends only on how one arranges the mechanism.

Consider now how the sign system of a natural language also has the above three properties. The finite set of discrete signs of a natural language consists of the sounds, combinations of sounds, and arrangements of sounds that recur in samples of messages in that language. These signs constitute what may be called the *expression system* of the language. They have a referential function in the sense that signs show consistent correspondences or relationships to states of affairs other than themselves—states of affairs either in objective reality, in the psychological state of the speaker, or in the message in which they appear. The set of correspondences between the signs of a language and such states of affairs may be called the *content system* of the language, or simply, the *meaning system* of the language.

Signs show various degrees of relationship with objective reality. There is little trouble defining the class of objects or events to which a word like *telephone* refers, but it may be difficult to identify the referents of words like *jealousy, teach, concept.* Some signs, like *Hi* and *Thanks* bear referential relationship only to certain kinds of social situations. Other signs refer to relations between referents; words like *in, of,* and *and* have this function. The particular sequential arrangement of signs may have a referential function; this is evident in the comparison of the strings *man bites dog* and *dog bites man.* The word *to* in an infinitive phrase like *to be* may be said to refer to something in the grammatical structure of the sentence in which it appears.

Still other signs, namely, the basic sound elements of a language (phonemes, to be discussed in Chapter 2), have no referential function in themselves, but constitute the component parts of other signs that do have referential meaning; frequently, these basic signs carry critical differences between referential signs. For example, the words *bin* and *pin* in English might be the same were it not that we discriminate their initial sounds. The two words *permit* (noun) and *permit* (verb) are differentiated by their patterns of stress or accent.

Finally, the ways in which the expression system of a particular language corresponds to its content system are essentially arbitrary. There is no reason, other than a historical one, why *pin* stands for a small pointed object instead of a storage receptacle. That two languages might happen to use two highly similar signs for the same referent could be a pure coincidence; usually the signs are quite different. There are cases, of course, where language signs seem not to be wholly arbitrary, as where expressions imitate animal cries or where they appear to exhibit what is known as *phonetic symbolism.* In cases of phonetic symbolism, the particular sounds of a word are presumably in some way correlated with the meaning of the word. For instance, it has been claimed that the meaning "smallness" is associated with the vowel sounds in such words as *little, teeny, pin, nip,* whereas "largeness" is associated with the vowel sounds in such words as *large, huge, pool, ocean,* and so on. But even though people show some consistency in their affective responses to pure sounds or nonsense syllables, the role of anything like phonetic symbolism in word formation or in carrying meaning is difficult to demonstrate. And even if phonetic symbolism is a significant factor, the essentially arbitrary character of signs still remains. The variations in words for animal cries in different languages are startling—compare, for example, *gnaf-gnaf* in French with *bow-bow*.[5]

The sign systems of natural languages exhibit a high degree of complexity in their structure, even though complexity is not an essential feature of a sign system. In the next chapter we shall explore this fact and its implications.

[5] For a representative recent study of phonetic symbolism, see M. S. Miron, *J. abnorm. soc. Psychol.,* 1961, 62, 623–630.

The Nature of Language

A language is a socially institutionalized sign system. It is the result of centuries of gradual development and change at the hands of many generations of speakers, but at any one point of history it exists as a set of patterns of behavior learned and exploited in varying degrees by each member of the speech community in which it is used. In studying the structure of a language we study the characteristics of these behavior patterns.

The behavioral science that concerns itself with the description and study of languages as sign systems is *descriptive linguistics*. Because of the rigor of its method-

8

2

ology and the precision of its results, descriptive linguistics is one of the most advanced of the behavioral sciences; even so, the description of a language system still presents many fundamentally unsolved problems.

If a psychologist were asked to describe the characteristics of a sign system as a set of behavior patterns, his first impulse would probably be to attempt to discover regular correspondences between stimuli and responses. He would try to find out what words the speakers of a language have learned to speak in given situations, and what responses these speakers would make to given words. That is, he would try to find correspondences between the content system of a language and its expression system.

The immediate results of such an approach would probably be quite trivial. They might consist of little more than a list of facts such as what one might predict by studying a dictionary. They would not begin to describe the ultimate structure of the total sign system. For one thing, the weight of evidence suggests that, except perhaps in limited cases, the correspondences between the content and the expression systems of a language are extremely complex. But more importantly, such an approach would be fraught with the danger that the description of the expression system would be made to depend on, or be biased by, the description of the content system. This is precisely the kind of mistake that has often been made in traditional grammar. For example, the definition of the grammatical category called *noun* has sometimes been made to depend on a conceptual classification of the things presumably symbolized by nouns: "persons, places, things, and abstract ideas." You can doubtless find many reasons why such a definition is unsatisfactory.

Descriptive linguistics has found it necessary to adopt a very different approach, namely, the concentrated study and description of the expression system *prior* to any attempt to coordinate it with the content system. A completely rigorous description of the expression system of a language must make no appeal to anything we ordinarily call "meaning." It is not denied that this expression system is, or may be, connected with a system of meanings, but the statement of the former must be independent of any statements about the latter. In most of this chapter we shall be talking about expression systems of languages: The question of their relationships to content systems will be postponed to the end of the chapter, or alluded to only briefly by suggesting what kinds of linguistic items are "meaningful."

THE STRUCTURE OF LANGUAGE: OVERVIEW

The basic problem of the linguist has been to develop a description of the sign system of a language, particularly its *expression* aspect (in the sense defined previously), from whatever materials he finds relevant for the purpose. In doing so he finds it necessary to adopt some theory or model of language structure, if only to have some categories into which to classify the findings. Historically, these models were at first fairly simple; they became more elaborate and refined as more and more languages were studied, and more and more aspects of languages were investigated. It was recognized from the very start, however, that models of language developed on the basis of such Western languages as English and Latin would not necessarily serve for the description of non-Western languages. (We avoid calling any language "primitive"; even the languages of "primitive" tribes have often proved to be fully as complex, at least in structure, as languages familiar to Western civilization.)

It is obvious that the raw material of which language signs are composed is *sound*. The first thing that the linguistic field worker does is to write down the speech uttered by his informant, initially in great detail in order not to miss anything that might be significant. In order to do so, the linguist has to be an expert in *phonetics,* the science of speech sounds, because it is frequently the case that the languages he studies present types of speech sounds unknown in the more familiar languages. The detailed record of the speech sounds composing a text is known as a *phonetic transcription.* Some linguists use for this purpose the list of symbols provided by the International Phonetic Alphabet (IPA); others modify this drastically, or make up their own symbols.

Having a phonetic transcription of his text before him, and possibly a rough translation, the linguist next tackles the job of teasing out the structure of the language. He would remember that a fundamental characteristic of a sign system is that it has a finite set of discrete, distinctive signs. The three general kinds of signs that the linguist would look for are these (each kind will be explained in more detail later):

1. *Distinctive basic sounds*—the types of sounds (vowels, consonants, tones or pitches, relative intensities, and durations or pauses) that are not meaningful in themselves but go to make up and differentiate the signs of a language, which may in turn have some sort of meaning or grammatical function. They are called *phonemes.*

2. *Forms*—sequences (not always continuous, however) of phonemes that constitute the basic grammatically functioning elements of a language. Some forms are very short, perhaps composed of a single phoneme, like the form that converts *dog* to *dogs* or *cat* to *cats.* Medium-sized forms are those that we ordinarily think of as words, like *dog, exercise, abracadabra.* Other forms can be longer than words, like the form *go through with,* because this is a set pattern whose meaning cannot be predicted from the separate words. Many forms appear in different "phonemic shapes" depending on the context in which they appear; in fact this is true of the plural-forming element just mentioned, because in *dogs* the form appears as the phoneme /z/ and in *cats* it appears as /s/. (For meaning of slant lines, see footnote 2, page 14.)

3. *Constructions*—patterns or arrangements of forms, the particular forms composing them being replaceable with other forms. An example is the noun phrase construction composed of a modifier and a head noun, illustrations of which are the noun phrases *green cheese, green hat, this hat, this car, this green car,* etc. The grammatical function of a construction will generally depend on the classes of forms that can compose it. In order to study constructions, one must have made an appropriate classification of forms.

This model of language implies that language structure is hierarchical. Constructions are composed of forms, and forms in turn are composed of distinctive basic sounds, or phonemes. In fact there can be a multiplicity of levels in the hierarchy: Forms can be combined to make other forms, and constructions can be combined to make still other constructions.

The general procedure of linguistic analysis has been to work "from the bottom up." In theory, the linguist's first task is to identify the phonemes; having done so, he identifies forms, and in turn, constructions. In practice, it is difficult to identify phonemes until at least some tentative identifications of forms have been made; each part of the analysis is continually revised in the light of findings in other parts until a satisfactory total description of the language is built up.

THE RAW MATERIALS OF LANGUAGE: SOUNDS

The varieties of sounds people can produce are very large in number— far larger than occur in any one language. *Phonetics* (to be carefully distinguished from *phonemics*) is the study and description of the varieties of sound that occur or can occur in different languages and their dialects. Phoneticians study the physical attributes of speech sounds, the manner in which they are produced by the human speech mechanism, and (sometimes) the manner in which they are perceived and discriminated by hearers.

Speech sounds can be classified by the ways they are produced. Vowels are produced by shaping the oral and nasal cavities in such a way that the sound issuing from the vocal cords or the windpipe has certain resonance qualities. Vowels can be roughly classified by noting the positions of the jaws, tongue, lips, and pharynx (which controls access of air to the nasal cavity). For example, the vowel [i] [1] in the English word *pin* is classified as an unrounded medial high front oral vowel, because in producing it the lips are unrounded, the highest part of the tongue is toward the front of the mouth and in a medium high position, and it is not nasalized. Consonants are produced when some part of the speech apparatus presents some degree of interference with the passage of air from the windpipe; the major variables that distinguish consonants from one another are (1) the point of articulation (the place in the mouth where the greatest interference occurs, and the surfaces involved), (2) voicing (that is, whether a voice tone accompanies the articulation), and (3) the type of articulation (the kind and degree of interference that occurs). Take, for instance, the initial [p] in the English word *pat*. The point of articulation is between the two lips, thus it is *bilabial*; the articulation is not simultaneously accompanied by a voice tone, hence it is *voiceless*; it is made by suddenly releasing the lips from a completely closed, or stopped, position to an open position, with a slightly noisy expulsion of air, hence it is an *aspirated stop*. In contrast, [v] in *vat* is a labiodental voiced fricative because the point of articulation is between the lower lip and the upper teeth, it is accompanied by a voice tone, and there is air friction. Study of articulatory phonetics will enable the student to produce a variety of sounds not found in English; for example, the sound of the *b* in Spanish *caballo*, often symbolized [β], is a *bilabial* voiced fricative, because the point of articulation is between the upper and lower lips.

---

[1] It is a convention in linguistics that a symbol enclosed in brackets is to be considered simply as a sound, that is, solely from the standpoint of phonetics.

Modern technology has made great contributions to the study of the physical attributes of sounds. Sound waves themselves can be portrayed with an oscilloscope (Figure 1). In addition, the sound spectrograph, which electronically plots the frequencies of the overtones in a sound wave against time (Figure 2), has made it possible to establish beyond question that vowel quality is directly correlated with the relative positions, on the frequency scale, of two or three *formants,* or bands of strong resonance overtones, present in the frequency spectrum of a sound. For example, regardless of the fundamental pitch at which it is spoken, the vowel [i] in *pin* is produced by a male adult speaker of English when he shapes his oral cavity so that the principal formants, or resonance bands, are at about 250 and 2100 cycles per second. A so-called "pattern playback device" has made it possible to find out what kinds of sounds are perceived when given combinations and sequences of formants are generated electromechanically. This device has shown that many of the stop consonants (like [p], [t], and [k]) have quite different acoustic characteristics depending on what vowel sounds they precede or follow. Through careful cutting and splicing of magnetic tape, one can demonstrate that a [k] sound before the diphthong [iy] (as in *key*) will sound like [p] when grafted on in front of the diphthong [uw] (as in *pool*). These findings raise the interesting psychological question of how two [k] sounds can be perceived as being the same or similar when their acoustic characteristics may be quite different. One possible answer is that we learn to perceive sounds in terms of the way we articulate them; it is as if we automatically refer any heard sound to the nerves and muscles that produce them.

PHONEMES

When we turn to the study of how sounds function in making up the distinctive signs of a language system, we realize, first, that a given language system uses only selected parts of the total range of possible speech sounds,

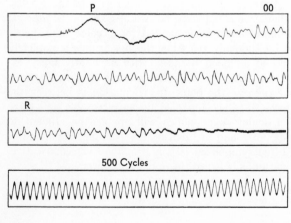

Figure 1.· A representation of the sound wave of the word poor, *with the wave of a 500-cycle tone for comparison. (From H. Fletcher.* Speech and hearing in communication. *Princeton: Van Nostrand, 1953, p. 33.)*

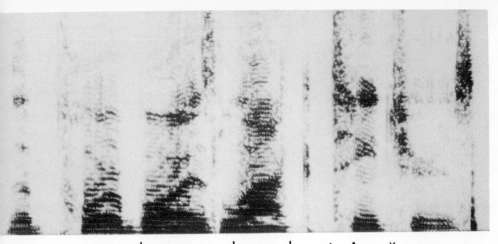

ðə p u w r b o y z l æ k t i y č ə r z

Figure 2. A sound spectrograph representation of the sentence The poor
boys lack teachers. *(Courtesy H. L. Cramer, Laboratory for Research in
Instruction, Harvard University.)*

and second, that sounds function as signs only as the users of a language learn
to recognize and produce differences in sounds that will produce differences
in the communicative values of the linguistic forms these sounds go to make
up.

A concrete illustration may help you understand this very important statement more fully. Start with the observation that one can generate a large
variety of hissing sounds—the kind of sound we ordinarily represent by the
letter "s." The tongue-tip can be placed in various positions—just back of
the teeth, or next to the gums, or even quite far back near the roof of the
mouth—and the rest of the tongue may assume various positions. Speakers
of English would probably perceive most of these sounds as "s" sounds;
any one of them could be used in pronouncing a word like *sin,* though some
of them might be perceived as producing the words *shin* or *thin.* Nevertheless,
the range of tongue positions that are ordinarily used for the "s" sound in
English is relatively narrow. But the total range of possible English "s"
sounds includes *two* ranges of "s" sounds for speakers of Arabic—one produced with the tongue just back of the upper teeth, and one produced with
the tongue-tip somewhat farther back and with the back of the tongue raised.
Although these two ranges of "s" sound are clearly discriminable by Arabic
speakers, speakers of English have great difficulty in distinguishing them
without training.

In linguistics, *phoneme* is a technical term for a range of sounds that the
speakers of a given language perceive as functionally the same and discriminate from other ranges of sound. Thus, within the range of sounds that are
perceived as "s" by English speakers, there is *one* phoneme in English, but
there are *two* phonemes in Arabic.

Phonemes are the building blocks out of which meaningful or grammatically
functional forms are composed; furthermore, they provide the critical basis

TABLE 1

English Phonemes and Some Words and Sentences Exemplifying Them (As in the Author's Dialect)

33 SEGMENTAL PHONEMES

20 Consonants		4 Semivowels	
		As Consonant	*In Diphthong*
Occurring as initial, medial, or final:			
/b/ as in *buy*	/s/ as in *so*		
/d/ as in *do*	/t/ as in *toe*	/h/ as in *hoe*	bah /bah/
/f/ as in *foe*	/v/ as in *vow*		
/g/ as in *go*	/z/ as in *zoo*	/r/ as in *roe*	err /ər/
/k/ as in *key*	/θ/ as in *thigh*		
/l/ as in *lie*	/ð/ as in *thy*	/w/ as in *woe*	now /naw/
/m/ as in *my*	/š/ as in *show*		
/n/ as in *no*	/č/ as in *chow*	/y/ as in *you*	boy /boy/
/p/ as in *pay*	/ǰ/ as in *Joe*		
Occurring only as medial or final:			
/ž/ as in *pleasure, rouge*			
/ŋ/ as in *singer, thing*			

9 Vowels

Simple Vowel + Consonant	*Followed by Semivowels*				
	/-y/	/-w/	/-h/	/-r/	/-yr/
/i/ as in *pit*	pea	*	*	*	pier
/e/ as in *pet*	pay	*	*	*	pare
/æ/ as in *pat*	*	*	/æh/ †	*	*
/ɨ/ as in *roses*	*	*	*	*	*
/ə/ as in *putt, but*	*	*	/əh/ **	purr ††	*
/a/ as in *pot*	pie	now	pa	par	pyre
/u/ as in *put, look*	buoy	coo	boo!	poor	*
/o/ as in *	boy	low	oh!	pore	*
/ɔ/ as in *	*	*	law	war	*

* Does not occur as a monosyllable in the author's Lower Connecticut Valley dialect, but may occur in other dialects of English.

† An interjection of frustration or disgust.

** The hesitation form.

†† In the author's dialect, this is a single *r*-like vowel, but it fits best into the pattern if considered a diphthong with /ə/.

for differentiating among these forms. One way in which we can identify the phonemes of a language is to try to find pairs of forms (words, for example) that speakers will identify as different in meaning or in use, but phonetically the same except for one sound. Such are called *minimal pairs*. For example, in English the words *Sam* and *sham* are a minimal pair that establishes the

4 Pitches: /¹/ (lowest), /²/, /³/, /⁴/ (highest).
4 Stresses: /´/ (primary), /ˆ/ (secondary), /`/ (tertiary), /˘/ (weak).
4 Junctures: /+/ (internal), /|/ (level), /||/ (rising), /#/ (falling, terminal).

A SAMPLE TRANSCRIPTION

He: /²dìjə + sîyðə + ³hwáythàws³||/
She: /²nów³||²kə̀zay + wɔ̀hntid + tə + vîzitðə + smìθsôwniyən + myùw³zíyəm²|
    ²ðə + lâybrərìyəv + ³káhŋgrìs³|²ǽnðə + jêfərsən + mə³móhriyəl²||
    ⁴ṣhl²|²in + tûw + ⁴áwrz²#/
He: /²ìm⁴páhsibəl¹#/

> *He:* Didja see the White House?
> *She:* No, 'cause I wanted to visit the Smithsonian Museum, the Library of Congress, and the Jefferson Memorial—(*excitedly*) all in two hours!
> *He:* (*incredulously*) Impossible!

sounds "s" and "sh" as different phonemes.[2] In Syrian Arabic the two words *saam* (a proper name) and *ṣaam* ("fasted") can be distinguished by an Arab speaker both in sound and in meaning (even though they might be indistinguishable to a speaker of English); this minimal pair establishes /s/ and /ṣ/ as different phonemes in Arabic, the two ranges of hissing sounds mentioned on p. 13. It is not always possible to find minimal pairs for all pairs of phonemes, but other kinds of evidence can be adduced to establish the list of phonemes for any particular language or dialect.

The student who plans to do practical work in any branch of psychology in which precise specification of speech stimuli and responses is required would do well to become aware of the phonemes of his own language, or better still, his particular dialect. He should also learn to make a phonemic transcription of his own speech. Table 1 gives a list of the phonemes found in the author's dialect of American English, as symbolized in one widely used transcription system; it also gives a sample phonemic transcription of a hypothetical conversation. A phonemic transcription represents only the sound units that are distinctive in the language being transcribed, and requires only the number of symbols that corresponds to the number of phonemes: It does not necessarily have to use the symbols of the International Phonetic Alphabet.

[2] Caution: the letters "sh" here stand for one sound, that is, one phoneme. It would perhaps be wiser to introduce phonemic symbols for the sounds of "s" and "sh": /s/ and /š/, respectively. The slant lines are used to indicate that what is enclosed in them is to be regarded as *phonemic,* as opposed to square brackets [ ] which enclose material regarded as merely *phonetic.*

The Nature
of Language

Segmental phonemes include consonants, vowels, and semivowels (phonemes that function either as consonants or as parts of diphthongs, like /w/ and /y/); they constitute the sequential segments (though with some overlapping and gliding) of syllables, words, and sentences. For example, the word *strokes* consists of the seven segmental phonemes /strowks/.

Suprasegmental phonemes include phonemes of stress, pitch, and juncture which occur simultaneously with the segmental phonemes or which separate them. Here, "stress" refers to the relative degree of intensity with which a syllable is pronounced; in English, four such degrees can be distinguished. Compare:

> I am còntént.
> It is devoid of cóntênt.
> The table of cóntènts. (In some dialects.)
> Satisfaction and cònténtmĕnt.[3]

Pitch refers to the relative height of the tone with which a syllable is spoken, or to some contour of such tones. Again, four pitch phonemes can be distinguished in English; see the sample transcription in Table 1. In Mandarin Chinese, the four tone contours with which syllables can be spoken generally indicate different meanings: Four possible meanings of the syllable *ch'i*, depending on tone, are "seven," "period of time," "rise," and "breath." *Juncture* refers to different types of transition between syllables or between clauses. The difference between the words *nitrate* and *night-rate* is a matter of whether a slight break, called an open transition and symbolized / + /, occurs between the phonemes /t/ and /r/. The differences between the following three pronunciations of "yes" are carried by intonation and juncture phonemes (it is hoped that the context and punctuation will suggest the pronunciation adequately):

> "Definitely; *yes!*"   /³yés¹#/
> ". . . . Yes, ... Yes, ..."   /²yés‖/ (said on the telephone by a speaker at intervals while he listens to the person at the other end of the line)
> "Well, what do you say? Yes?"   /³yés‖/

Even a simple utterance like the "m-hm" which is sometimes used in psychological experiments to indicate approval (constituting "reinforcement," allegedly) can be said in a rather large variety of ways, but it is possible to standardize this utterance if the speaker will stick to a given contour of stresses, intonations, and junctures. A good contemporary textbook of linguistics, or better still, an expert on the linguistics of English, should be consulted for details.[4]

Phonemes are essentially classes or categories of sound; variation and intergradation within a phoneme class can occur. Some of this variation is free,

---

[3] An interesting function of stress that the author has observed is its "honorific" use in indicating that something is "well-known," "famous." An ordinary person on the street might be named Clárk Gáble, just like Jóhn Dóe. But make him a movie star and you have Clàrk Gáble. Similarly, compare Ábrahàm Líncoln, Âbrahàm Líncoln; whíte hóuse, Whíte Hòuse; Thírd Âvenue, Fífth Ávenue.

[4] See Selected Readings, p. 113.

some of it conditioned. For example, a person could freely use any of several varieties, or *allophones*, of /s/ in the word *span*, but the difference between the /p/ of *span* and that of *pan* is conditioned by whether a pause or a sibilant precedes it. Phonetically, these two allophones of the /p/ phoneme are distinguished by the fact that in *span*, /p/ is *un*aspirated, whereas in *pan* it is aspirated. You can feel the difference if you hold your palm about two inches in front of the mouth as you say these words. This conditioned variation is by no means inevitable: It is possible to pronounce *pan* with the unaspirated allophone (it will sound almost like *ban*, as if spoken with a French accent) or to pronounce *span* with the aspirated allophone (it will sound "funny," perhaps as if spoken with a German accent). The way English speakers pronounce *pan* and *span* is just a matter of learning; the complexity of this learning process should not, however, be underestimated. That this learning is automatic and unconscious is suggested by the occurrence of the expected variation in allophones even when English speakers are asked to pronounce two completely new words like *pown* and *spown* There are many other cases of conditioned variation in phonemes in English; indeed, such variation occurs in every language.

Usually, the phonemes of a language can be classified phonetically so as to exhibit a neat structure (see Table 2). For example, all voiced consonant pho-

TABLE 2

Chart of Some English Consonant Phonemes *

Place of Articulation †	Type of Articulation †								
	Stop V−	V+	Nasal (V+)	Fricative V−	V+	Affricate V−	V+
Bilabial	p	b	m				
Labiodental				f	v		
Dental				θ	ð		
Alveolar	t	d	n	s	z		
Alveopalatal				š	ž	č	ǰ
Velar	k	g	ŋ				

V−: Voiceless
V+: Voiced
* To avoid complications, the semivowels r, y, w, and h and the lateral l have been omitted.
† The meanings of terms such as *alveolar, fricative,* etc., can be found in most standard dictionaries, or you can attempt to infer these meanings from the characteristics of the sounds themselves. For the meaning of the phonemic symbols, see Table 1.

nemes in English except the nasals have voiceless counterparts. This and other facts about phonemes may be explained by the theory that each phoneme represents a group of *distinctive features* present in a single sound. Voicing, for example, is such a feature, which in English is present in all vowels and a certain group of consonants.

After a linguist has identified the phonemes of the language he is studying, he goes on to establish the forms that constitute grammatically functional signs in a language. *Form* is a general term for any linguistic unit with definite (though possibly varying) phonemic content. Here are some forms in English, presented in their conventional spellings:

good	get	un-
-ness	forget	re-
goodness	forget-me-not	construct
for goodness' sake		-ed
	hot	unreconstructed
berry	house	
mulberry	hothouse	go through with

Some of these are smaller than what we call "words"; [5] they are called *bound* forms because they never occur alone. Others are words, or combinations of words; these are termed *free* forms because they can occur alone. Every form given, however, has a definite and distinct grammatical function. For example, *-ness* has an essentially grammatical function; when added as a suffix, it changes the grammatical use of words like *good, thorough,* and *connected* in a consistent way. Forms like *good, forget, construct,* and *hothouse,* however, have not only grammatical functions, but also correspondences to certain events and attributes of reality as perceived by human beings.

The identification of these forms by techniques of linguistic analysis is not easy. The mere fact that a certain string of phonemes occurs with high regularity is not enough to establish it as a linguistic form, and we have pointed out that appeal to "meaning" is not reliable. Some of the questions that might arise, with the answers that would probably be rendered by linguistic analysis, are the following: Is *mul* in *mulberry* a form? (Probably not.) Is the form *for* in *for goodness' sake* the same form as the first syllable of *forget*? (No.) Can the first syllables of *forget* and *forsake* be regarded as a distinct form? (Probably not in present-day English.) Is the syllable /liš/ occurring in *English, establish, girlish,* and *delicious* the same form? (No, except that /-iš/ in *English* is the same form as that in *girlish.*) Is *un-* in *unreconstructed* the same form as *un* in *uncovered*? (Yes, but only if *uncovered* is the form that means "not covered" rather than "revealed.") Ascertaining these answers without appeal to the specific meanings of the forms is no mean trick; linguists believe they can do it, however, solely by examining and comparing the sequences in which the phonemes appear, or the ways in which the forms are built.

It is difficult, also, to know whether to regard any given sequence of forms as being itself a form, that is, a unit. We could argue that *forget-me-not* is a unit because it can replace *flower* in most constructions, and because it is not

[5] It is very difficult to define *word* as a linguistic concept; the linguist cannot accept the conventions of spelling, whereby "words" are separated by spaces, as evidence for what is to be regarded as a word.

likely that any comparable form (for example, *forget-thee-not*) would be freely constructed. *For goodness' sake* is a more debatable case; it has some of the earmarks of a construction (see below) since various other forms can be freely substituted for *goodness*. On the other hand, the form is always an exclamation or a parenthetical expression; it always has the shape *for ......* *sake;* and its meaning has little to do with its specific content. I am inclined to call it a form. You may want to consider whether *go through with* ought to be regarded as a form.

Any form that cannot be divided into two or more other forms is a *morpheme*. *Good, -ness, get, forget, un-, re-, construct, -ed, hot, house, berry, mulberry* in the above list are all morphemes. (*Forget* and *construct* had two morphemes in the languages from which they came, Anglo-Saxon and Latin, respectively, but they do not have two morphemes in present-day English.)

Like phonemes, morphemes can exhibit both free and conditioned variation. The morpheme *-ing* in *working, being,* and so forth shows more or less free variation with *-in'*. (At least, a speaker could say *working* in some situations and *workin'* in others; any variables that control this would be extralinguistic.) But the pluralizing suffixes spelled *-s, -es, -en, -i,* in *rocks, dogs, roses, oxen,* and *alumni* and pronounced /-s, -z, -ɨz, -ɨn, -ay *or* -iy/ can be thought of as conditioned variants of a single morpheme which may be symbolized {Z}. The study of forms constitutes the branch of grammatical analysis called *morphology.*

CONSTRUCTIONS

Morphemes do not just get strung out one after the other in any order whatsoever.[6] *Sake for ness good* or *Is well John very* might cause some puzzlement, even though they might serve as items on intelligence tests. The branch of grammar that deals with the arrangement of forms into acceptable sequences is *syntax.*

In the most general terms, acceptable sequences occur in what may be called *constructions.* Constructions are patterns in which forms can be placed; they themselves are empty of specific phonemic or morphemic content. If we start with the words *He went* we can replace *He* with such words and phrases as *I, Al,* or *Alice's sister,* and *went* with such words and phrases as *coughed* and *said that it was raining,* still preserving the basic construction. In fact, a construction is a series of "slots" into which particular kinds of material can be fitted. But each slot must contain a particular kind of material; if it does not, the result either belongs to another construction (*I Caesar* is not the same construction as *I coughed*) or is not accepted as meaningful by the speakers of the language (*I very* is not an acceptable construction in English). The

---

[6] For that matter, neither do phonemes. The patterns in which phonemes occur are peculiar to each language, and quite rigid. The phoneme /ŋ/ never occurs at the beginning of a word or syllable in English, although a comparable phoneme does occur as a syllable-initial in many other languages. Nor does the sequence /vtsr/ appear in English, although there is no phonetic reason why it couldn't. Naive subjects asked to make up new words or spoken nonsense syllables almost always unwittingly conform to the phonemic patterns of their language.

slots may contain single forms, or they may contain still other constructions. Sometimes a slot can be left unfilled, in which case its content is called "zero." A construction is like a recipe, or a computer program, as if it said, for example, "Take anything in Class M, follow it with anything in Class 47, then finish off with something from Class N." Thus, as was said previously, in order to describe constructions we must be able to identify the classes of things that can go into their slots. Some of these classes are called form-classes, corresponding roughly to what have been traditionally been called parts of speech. Constructions, too, fall into classes.

Here, for example, are six groups of phrases or sentences, each group illustrating a particular kind of construction in English. In each group, there are four examples, and in every case, the first two have single forms as their components, while the last two may introduce further constructions substituted for one or more of these forms.

(1)	(2)	(3)
He sings	pay attention	women and children
Demolition occurred	have fun	either you or I
The five boys chose Jim	have had measles	both the Republicans and the Democrats
Women and children should be allowed to leave first	mention the fact that he came	big ones and little ones

(4)	(5)	(6)
was sick	sick men	year after year
seemed green	consistent evidence	beer after beer
appeared to be neither consistent nor plausible	the red, white, and blue flag	layer on layer
proved to be innocent of this crime	old newspapers and books	sleepless night after sleepless night

A good deal of the grammar of a language can be formulated in terms of *phrase structure grammar*. The principal tool of this kind of grammar is the *rewrite rule*. This has the general form $X \rightarrow Y$, which is read, "X is to be rewritten as Y," where X is any construction or a component of one, and Y is an expansion of X or its replacement by a particular form. For example, we can start with the prescription for one of the primary types of sentence:

Sentence $\rightarrow$ Subject + Predicate

and successively derive particular sentences by using such rewrite rules as

Subject $\rightarrow$ Noun, Pronoun, or Noun Phrase
Predicate $\rightarrow$ Verb, or Verb Phrase
Noun Phrase $\rightarrow$ Determiner + Noun
Verb Phrase $\rightarrow$ Verb + Noun Phrase
Determiner $\rightarrow$ *a, the, this, that, some*

Noun → *man, boy, book, train*
Verb → *read, stopped, drank*

to yield such sentences as

1. A man read the book.
2. The boy stopped the train.
3. Some train read a man.
4. A train drank a book.

(The rewrite rules given above are not complete; they are only illustrative. The actual rewrite rules for the phrase structure grammar of English would be much more complicated.) Not all these sentences are meaningful, but they are all "grammatical" in the sense that they conform to the rules. It is possible to formulate rules that will exclude "nonsense" sentences like (3) and (4) above; the only problem is to know how far it is wise to carry such a procedure.

Consider, now, the following sentences:

1. You solved those problems.
2. You didn't solve those problems.
3. *Those* problems you solved, *these* you didn't.
4. Didn't you solve those problems?
5. Those problems weren't solved by you.
6. Solve those problems!
7. How you solved those problems!

Sentence 1 is clearly a "rewrite" from the basic construction Sentence → Subject + Predicate. *You* is a subject, *solved those problems* is a predicate derived from Predicate → Verb + Noun Phrase; Noun Phrase → Determiner + Noun.

We may now ask: Is sentence 2 a "rewrite" from 1 by the expansion of *solved* to *did solve* to *didn't solve*? Conceivably, yes, but there are several reasons why the intermediate step *did solve* is gratuitous and incorrect. Rather, the derivation of sentence 2 can best be regarded as a special kind of process in grammar called a *transformation*. Specifically, sentence 2 is a *negative* transformation of sentence 1. The sentence *You did solve those problems* would be regarded as a quite different transformation of 1, an *emphatic* transformation.

Sentence 3 would be even harder to derive from 1 by the usual rewrite rule, for elements are transposed. This would be called, in fact, a *transposed object* transformation. Sentence 4 introduces the *interrogative* transformation; in deriving this sentence, we must apply the negative transformation before the interrogative. The *passive* transformation is introduced in sentence 5, with a negative transformation applied; note that it would be awkward to derive sentence 5 directly from 2, since the *did* element would have to be deleted; it is neater to start with sentence 1, apply the passive transformation, and then the negative. Nevertheless, deletion of *You* to produce the *imperative* transformation in sentence 6 seems reasonable enough. Sentence 7 illustrates one variety of *exclamatory* transformation.

Thus, some constructions are *transformations* of other constructions; it is parsimonious to make a systematic study of these transformations in developing the grammar of a language.

Many morphological phenomena can be interpreted as transformations, also. Here are some examples:

Transformation	Of	Result
Put in past tense	take	took
Nominalize	good	goodness
Adjectivalize	wood	wooden
Verbalize	intense	intensify
Make past participle	cover	covered
Reverse action	cover	uncover
Make past participle	uncover	uncovered
Make negative	covered	uncovered

That *uncovered* can be produced by two different transformations, with two different meanings, illustrates a most interesting application of this approach to grammar. It can be applied to the interpretation of ambiguous sentences like the following:

They are frying chickens.

This sentence is a transformation either of *They fry chickens* or of *They are chickens for frying*. In actual use, the context would usually furnish the key to which of these transformations was intended by the author of the sentence. The point is that many "constructionally ambiguous" expressions cannot be analyzed satisfactorily without some reference to their "transformational history."

METHODOLOGICAL PROBLEMS IN LINGUISTIC ANALYSIS

The results of linguistic analysis, so briefly sketched here, have not been easily achieved, and there is still room for argument about the validity of these results. Linguists do not all work within the same theoretical and methodological frameworks. Some theories postulate that an exhaustive description of a language can be made solely by stating the items (phonemes, forms) of a language and their arrangements; other theories view language as a set of items to which various "processes" (such as transformations) can be applied to produce meaningful utterances. In either view, language is a formal set of facts that exist independently of people who might potentially use the language.

Many linguists have insisted, with some justice, on studying only language behavior that has actually been observed, instead of experimenting with patterns of behavior that might occur. They would not dream of asking an informant, "Would you say it this way?" (offering a postulated novel utterance), because this might bias the informant's judgment of the acceptability of the utterance.

Until recently, linguists have generally restricted themselves to studying the relatively long utterances of single speakers telling stories or giving reminiscences, and have paid insufficient attention to the speech of normal social interaction, with its fragmentary sentences, pauses, and rephrasings.

It is often said that the complete statement of the grammar of a language (that is, a description of all the form-classes, constructions, and grammatical processes found in the language, with all their variants) would fill a very large volume. This seems paradoxical when the claim has been made, as it has indeed, that a child of normal intelligence "knows" all the essential grammatical structure of his language by the time he is six years old, if not before. Either the feat of the child is actually greater than we think it is, or there is something wrong with the assertion that a grammar of a language needs to be voluminous.

Of course, the feat of a child in learning his native language *is* impressive, but it would seem that these learnings could be listed and described in something less bulky than a Bible-sized grammatical treatise! How can we state the child's "knowing" of grammatical structure? Knowledge of grammatical structure has two aspects: First, aside from certain problems of vocabulary and sheer grammatical complexity, a six-year-old is capable, we are told, of understanding any utterance by a speaker of the language, even though he has never heard it before; and second, he is capable of uttering sentences that will be accepted as meaningful and "grammatical" by other speakers of the language, even though those sentences may never have been said by anybody before. This capability of generating and understanding novel utterances is the essence of language; actually, the most valid objective of linguistic analysis is to describe this capability as a set of learned responses common to the users of a language. The attempt to describe linguistic structures solely on the basis of samples of text, divorced from the situations in which the texts were uttered or created, can never have more than a partial success.

In recent years, linguists have in fact been directing their attention more closely to the many varieties of normal speech pattern. C. C. Fries,[7] for example, was one of the first to point out the structural differences in what he called "situation sentences" (those that could begin a conversation), "sequence sentences" (those that continue a conversation without change of speaker), and "response sentences" (utterances that continue a conversation, but by a new speaker). These are illustrated, respectively, as follows:

1. Speaker A: I'm going to take the car for a grease-job.
2. Speaker A: Needs it pretty badly.
3. Speaker B: Yeah, prob'ly.

Noam Chomsky, a linguist, is chiefly responsible for the development of a theory of grammar that explicitly tries to formulate the phrase-structures, rewrite rules, and transformations that apply when a speaker of a language generates a novel utterance or accepts a presented novel utterance as "grammatical." He has emphasized the notion that linguistic analysis must provide

[7] C. C. Fries. *The structure of English.* New York: Harcourt, Brace & World, 1952.

a model for describing how speakers construct utterances, and how hearers can understand or "construe" them when they hear them.[8]

The linguistic analysis of English (or of any other language) is still far from complete. The objective is to be able to describe exhaustively all the constructions and transformations that function at the various levels of analysis—from the complete utterance, through the sentence, clause, and phrase, down to the smallest and most elementary linguistic form. If we are going to be able to account for the linguistic behavior of the user of a language we need a complete description of the linguistic patterns that are available to him as a speaker and that must be interpreted by him as a hearer. As psychologists we will be in a better position to utilize this information if it is stated in purely formal terms, that is, without appeal to the "meanings" of form-classes, constructions, and transformations, because the problem of meaning is better left for the psychologist to solve. The labels we put on form-classes and other categories may indeed suggest "meanings," but these labels could just as well be arbitrary. In fact, Fries has established four principal form-classes that he refuses to label as anything else than classes I, II, III, and IV, even though it is evident that they correspond fairly well with the classes we ordinarily call *nominals, verbals, adjectivals,* and *adverbials.*

If we analyze complete utterances, we will find the following types of expression units or expression-types:

I. Nonsentential expressions.
 A. Greetings, etc. *Hi, How-do-you-do, Goodbye, So long, "Over."*
 B. Calls and other attention getters (some of which can be inserted in sentences): *Hey! John! Well . . .* /əh/.
 C. Nonsentential exclamations: *Oh! Ouch! Golly! Damnation!*
 D. Nonsentential responses to another speaker: *Yes, no, O.K., m-hm, Thanks, "Roger."*
II. Sentence-types.
 A. Existence-assertions: The basic pattern is [*There* + a verb phrase], the verb phrase including some form of the verb *to be* or occasionally one of a small number of intransitive verbs (*come, occur, live*), plus a nominal. Example: *There is a problem here.*
 B. Predications: The basic pattern is: [Subject + Predicate], where Subject → Nominal; Predicate → one of the following constructions (all verb phrases):
  1. Linking verb + Nominal: "is his sister," "was Tuesday."
  2. Linking verb + Adjectival: "is sick," "was dedicated to truth."
  3. Linking verb + Adverbial: "is home," "is in Paris."
  4. Intransitive verb: "rains," "is swimming," "occurred," "exists."
  5. Transitive Verb + Object(s): "killed a rabbit," "received a letter," "gave him money," "elected him president."

The major transformations that apply to sentence-types and leave them still in the form of sentences or minimal utterances are the following:

[8] See the excerpts from Chomsky that appear in *Psycholinguistics,* edited by S. Saporta, New York: Holt, Rinehart and Winston, 1961.

a. Null—the declarative sentence. (According to Chomsky, any sentence that has not been subjected to any transformation is a "kernel sentence.")
b. Negative.
c. Passive (applicable only to certain sentence-types containing a transitive verb and at least one object).
d. Formal interrogative: Interrogative sentences that may be "pivoted" on different components of a construction, sometimes on two or more, as in *"Who is going when in what vehicle?"*
  i. *Yes-no* questions: Pivoted on verb phrase. "Are you going?"
  ii. *Wh*-question: Pivoted on subject, object, indirect object, adverbial, or adjectival. "When are you going?"
e. Intonation question: Intonation contour applied to declarative sentence. "You went?"
f. Echo-question: Formal interrogative question of another speaker restated or rephrased with special intonation contour. Speaker B: "What are you doing?" Speaker A: "What am I doing?"
g. Transposition: Part of predicate transposed. *"Those* problems I solved."
h. Subject postponement (applies only to predications). "It is true that he is here" < "That he is here is true."
i. Imperative (applies only to predications). "Solve those problems."
j. Exclamation: Pivoted on different components of constructions, parallel to interrogative transformation.
k. Deletion: One or more components of a sentence-type may be deleted in "sequence" or "response" utterances when the content of the deletion is clear from preceding context.

By means of these lists, we can assign expression-types to the components of the following possible utterance:

Hi there, Bud. Listen! What I'd like to know is, what the dickens *is* your name?

Or we should be able to take a complex sentence like the following and analyze it as a complex series of constructions and expressions from basic sentence-types:

The mathematical concept that has attracted the most widespread attention from psychologists and linguists interested in communication theory is that of entropy.

Here, the basic expression-type to which this sentence reduces is a predication with a subject ("The mathematical concept . . . theory"), a linking verb ("is"), and a nominal ("that of entropy"). The subject is in turn a nominal phrase with a clause transformed from a predication with a transitive verb, of the form "Concept . . . attracted . . . attention," and this in turn contains a construction transformed from a predication with a linking verb and adjectival, of the form "Psychologists and linguists are interested in. . . ." We haven't space, of course, to give all the details of these processes.

The deletion transformation is particularly useful as a possible analysis of the many "fragmentary" utterances heard in normal conversation: "The bread, dear." "Needs more power." "By the door." In many cases, of course, it would be difficult to decide on the exact "transformational history" of such an utterance; for example, "By the door" could be derived from "It's by the door," or "You'll find it by the door," and so on. The point is that such abbreviated utterances can be referred back to basic types of utterances whose use and function can in theory be clearly described; it is not necessary to create a special grammar to take care of abbreviated or fragmentary utterances.

ANALYSIS OF THE CONTENT SYSTEM OF THE LANGUAGE

Throughout the preceding discussion of the expression system of language, we have tried to treat the problem of meaning as cautiously and as gingerly as the linguist does. We have emphasized the reasons why linguists feel it is necessary to study the expression system of a language independently of the content system. At the same time, we have not hesitated to give labels to various linguistic phenomena which will give some indication of their possible "meanings."

Even though linguists have often written about the desirability of making an analysis of the content system of a language, their scant progress in doing so is probably an indication that such an analysis would be impossible without drawing on information about the *use* of a linguistic system by the speakers of a language.

We can be sure that the meaning of a particular linguistic form or construction cannot be studied in isolation—that is, independently of a particular instance of its use—for it can have different meanings depending on the context. This idea from the *context theory* of meaning can be accepted, but we should recognize that the context does not necessarily *yield* the meaning of an item: It only provides a basis—sometimes shaky at that—for deciding which of a number of possible meanings it may have. A statement of this meaning is necessary, regardless of what information may be supplied by context.

Semantic analysis of a language would involve the listing of all its forms, constructions, and transformations and the giving for each one of these a statement of all the possible relationships it may have to the content system. In this way, the *denotations* (see p. 40) of these linguistic elements would be stated.

For example, suppose we are interested in stating the denotations of the morpheme /mæn/ and its variant /men/. To do this, we would need to collect a large number of instances in which this morpheme is used: We might find such instances as: *Man is mortal, Man the oars! Manning table. The child is father to the man. Five men came. Man-crazy.* Through a long process of asking informants to interpret these sentences, we might eventually arrive at an analysis something like this for *man* in *Man is mortal:* Grammatically, it is subject; the denotation of the construction is that something is "predicated" about this subject, or in view of the use of a linking verb and an adjectival, some "attribute" of "man" is offered. Also, grammatically it belongs to the form-class we call *nouns:* it is a "count-noun" because it may be preceded by the article *a*. The fact that no article precedes it at all, however, signals or denotes that it is to be taken "generically," that is, man in general rather than any particular man; in fact, it includes "woman." (*Man* is one of a very few nouns for which omission of the article signifies generic meaning. We cannot form the analogous expression "Automobile is expensive.") We finally come to the pure *lexical* denotation of /mæn/, namely, member of the human species. Similar analyses would have to be made for the other instances of /mæn/ in our sample until we could be sure that no new denotations could be found.

All forms, constructions, and processes have grammatical meaning, that is, meaning concerned with the constructions in which they are found or to which they may be applied. Most forms also have lexical content, that is, some kind of reference to states of affairs outside the utterance or text in which they are found. Some grammarians have claimed that lexical meaning is a property of only certain major parts of speech (nouns, verbs, adjectives, and adverbs), implying that the remaining parts of speech are "function words" with only grammatical meaning. But it is clear that many "function words" (for instance, prepositions like *in, on, with, despite*) have lexical components that are relatively easy to define.

Lexicography, which has been practiced for centuries, is the art of listing, in some rational order, all the items of a language with their meanings, or "definitions." Exactly what units are to be listed and how their meanings are to be defined have always been problems. Ideally, a dictionary should list all the morphemes, forms, and constructions that occur in a language. In practice, the lexicographer has usually taken the word as his unit. He will sometimes list compound words and forms like *forget-me-not* when they occur with high frequency in samples of the language or when their meanings cannot be predicted from their constituent forms. Ideally, also, each possible grammatical and lexical meaning for each item should be given, but in practice, the lexicographer tries to specify the various parts of speech (form-classes) in which a form may be found, and to indicate the "meanings" that are possible in each case. There are no absolute rules to follow in deciding how many entries should be made for a form, how many meanings a form has, or how those "meanings" should be stated. It is interesting, however, to study the practice of different dictionaries in these respects; they vary widely. It is for this reason that it is ill-advised to use any ordinary dictionary as a basis for developing methods for measuring vocabulary size, as some psychologists have tried to do.

The principal function of a dictionary "definition" is to provide information that will enable the user to fit the meaning and use of an unfamiliar word into the system of meanings he has already acquired. "Definitions" may contain synonyms, synonymous expressions, or reference to particular attributes of the item being defined. Typical contexts in which an item may be found are given (for example, "*strike:* in baseball, . . ."). That these procedures generally work reasonably well does as much credit to the user of a dictionary as to its maker.

Linguists do not attempt to legislate the grammar and structure of a language; they merely describe what they observe. Likewise, a dictionary does not attempt to set standards of usage or fix the meanings of words; it is only a repository of information concerning word usages of wide enough currency to be regarded as significant in the speech community at the time of publication.

We can go beyond the dictionary in studying the content system of a language. We can examine the total stock of lexical items for the number of distinctions that are made, and the number of subordinate and superordinate terms they contain in a given domain. For example, what are the items we have in English for persons of different ages and sexes? They may be represented as follows:

(Male)		(generalized)		(Female)
?	—	(oldster?)	—	?
man	—	adult	—	woman
(boy)	—	adolescent, teenager	—	(girl)
↕				↕
(boy)	—	child, "kid," youngster	—	(girl)
?	—	infant, baby	—	?

There are quite a few gaps in this grid. We have no separate and distinctive terms for babies, children, and adolescents of the two sexes, and no special terms at all, really, for old people. Compare Italian *bimbo* (boy-baby), *bimba* (girl-baby), Latin *senis*, old man.

On the other hand, English has a relatively rich vocabulary for colors and shades (*red, pink, orange, magenta,* and so on) in comparison to many other languages. It is of interest to study some of the distinctions offered by the lexicon of English: For example, what is denoted by the following words with the general meaning "give"—*grant, donate, contribute, bestow, present, bequeath, dispense, award*? The difference between *bestow* and *present* has partly to do with the relative social status of giver and receiver; such a difference is not mentioned in most dictionaries.

Making statements concerning the "denotation" of certain form-classes and constructions is difficult. For example, it is sometimes claimed that the meaning of the "subject" of a sentence like *the man swam* is "actor" and that of the verb is "action." This seems to be contradicted, however, in *Bob received a letter,* since Bob didn't have to "do" anything to receive a letter, nor is "receiving" an action. On the other hand, it may be noted that as the child learns language, nearly all the verbs he learns earliest (like *eat, bite, drop, pull, hit*) refer to definite actions. The "action" component of the verb form-class is so dominant that it is possible that it transfers to words like *have, receive,* and *owe,* which also belong to this form-class, in the sense that native speakers "feel" that *having, receiving,* and *owing* are in some way "actions."

LINGUISTICS AND PSYCHOLOGY

There are at least three points at which linguistics and psychology have clearly common interests. (We must remind ourselves that linguistics is essentially a behavioral science.)

One is the possibility of "universals" in grammar and in language structure. Anything that is universal in natural languages is likely to have psychological significance as a basic property of human communication. For example, it is probable that all languages have transformations in their grammar and that all languages have devices for asking questions. Thus far, unfortunately, linguists have made very little advance towards cataloging universal properties of languages.[9]

A second is the possibility of significant *differences* between languages in the kinds of relationship they exhibit between their expression and content systems, and the possible implications such differences may have for the cognitive behavior of the speakers of those languages. A small start has been made in investigating such differences; the results will be discussed in Chapter 7.

A third is the possibility of making a psychological interpretation of grammatical structure. Although linguists have justifiably avoided any appeal to psychological considerations, it is possible that the grammatical phenomena formally described by the linguist can be even more parsimoniously described in terms of what may be called their "psychological motivation" or "dynamic logic." That is to say, given a certain linguistic construction, we may be able to find a psychological motivation for its existence and to show its relationship to other constructions in a way that cannot be done by formal analysis. One justification for this assertion is that linguists have frequently found it necessary to re-do their analyses in the light of new discoveries. For example, the discovery of phonemes of stress, intonation, and juncture in the 1940's made it possible to make a thorough revision of treatments of morphology and syntax. Comparable discoveries in the psychological sphere could lead the way to still further revisions of statements of linguistic structure.

It seems clear that psychological analysis of linguistic behavior needs to proceed "from the top down" rather than "from the bottom up" as in usual linguistic procedures. In formulating an utterance, it is probable that a speaker selects its over-all construction (that is, its basic expression-types) rather than the particular words that will compose it, much less the phonemes of those words. The future task of psychological linguistic analysis, then, is to describe the situational and psychological concomitants and antecedents of the major expression-types listed on page 24. The processes by which these basic patterns are modified by "rewrite rules" and by transformations should then be studied from the point of view of psychological motivation. There is a real challenge in the task of determining whether these processes indeed have any psychological reality beyond the formal analysis produced so elegantly by linguists, and whether, therefore, these processes play a fundamental role in thought and action.

[9] The volume edited by Greenberg, listed in the Readings, may stimulate the interested student.

The Learning of Language

Many species of animals —ants, bees, birds, and wolves, among others—have systems of communication that have in rudimentary form some of the characteristics of human language. In one or more of these systems one can find such features as: use of the vocal apparatus, seemingly arbitrary signs, and means for communicating information, feelings, and emotions. However, these systems are for the most part passed on by heredity, unchanged from generation to generation, and they are all extremely simple.

Human language, in contrast, is always learned. Each child must learn his language from scratch, and the sur-

3

prising thing is how rapidly, relatively speaking, he picks up whatever language he is reared in (and how fast he can learn another language during his very early years). The only hereditary element in human language is that a normal child is born with the complex neural equipment he needs to learn and produce it. Despite patient efforts, it has thus far been impossible to teach primates (like chimpanzees) to speak more than a very few words, and then only with difficulty. This poor showing seems to be due partly to the primates' poorly developed neural equipment for controlling the speech musculature, and partly to the limitation of their capacity for handling a complex symbolic system. It may be noted, incidentally, that some animals (dogs, for example) have shown considerable capability in learning to respond differentially to a small vocabulary of words and phrases, but this is only what one might expect in view of the capacity of animals for discrimination learning.

THE COURSE OF LANGUAGE DEVELOPMENT IN THE CHILD

Relevant to the learning of language are at least three interrelated sequences of development: (1) "cognitive" development, that is, a child's capacity to recognize, identify, discriminate, and manipulate the features and processes of the world around him; (2) development of the capacity to discriminate and comprehend the speech he hears from others in his environment; and (3) development of ability to produce speech sounds and sequences of speech sounds that conform more and more closely to the patterns of adult speech. The last of these depends on the second, and both of them depend at least partly on the first. It is sometimes claimed that listening-comprehension ability also depends on the development of speech ability, and although this may be to some extent true, it is not a necessary dependency, as witnessed by the occasional case of a child who develops good listening comprehension without a corresponding ability to talk. The great dependency of speaking on hearing is demonstrated by the enormous difficulties encountered in teaching deaf children to speak in anything approaching a normal manner.

Actually, we have most information about the development of a child's speech responses; we know much less about the development of his ability to perceive and interpret speech, and still less about his cognitive development in the early years. In what follows, we pay primary attention to speech development; cognitive development is considered in Chapter 6.

The organically determined cries of an infant in the first two or three months gradually give way to the apparently random vocalization known as the "babbling stage." There is some ground for thinking that this stage is biologically determined, since it occurs in many babies who are subsequently found to be congenitally deaf. At the same time, the amount of babbling has a significant dependence on the presence of adults who reinforce this babbling. Although certain trends can be observed in the kinds of sounds emitted by an infant in the babbling stage, these sounds have little bearing on the phonemes of the language the child is to learn. In fact, some children virtually stop babbling when they begin to learn their first "words." It is at this point that true language development starts.

Even before the end of the babbling period, infants start to discriminate speech forms. Probably some of the first aspects of speech they learn to discriminate are certain basic stress and intonation patterns that communicate the feelings and desires of adults. But at about the age of 11 months they start learning to obey simple verbal commands, and we may infer that they can begin to respond to the total phonemic configuration of words and phrases.

Doubtless these discriminations stand them in good stead when they start to learn to produce real speech themselves, typically around 12 months of age. The process by which a child learns the phonology, vocabulary, and grammar of his language is actually fairly long and arduous; even though progress may appear to be rapid, there is a very great deal to learn. All aspects of development progress simultaneously and are interrelated.

A child learns the phonemes of his language through a process of gradual differentiation. Initially, the words he speaks may seem to have only an approximate similarity to the words in the adult language that they presumably imitate, but the evidence suggests that even at this stage *the child has a phonemic system of his own,* even though rudimentary. For example, a child who pronounces *car, cat,* and *cup* as /tah, tæt, təp/ has only one phoneme, /t/, where the adult language has two, /k, t/. It may be several years before the child's phonemic system on the production side approximates that of the adult language. According to one theory of child language development (that of the linguist Roman Jakobson), the gradual differentiation of a child's phonemic system is correlated with the manner in which he acquires the various distinctive features contained in phonemes (see p. 17).

The vocabulary development of a child is at first rather slow; six months after he has said his first "meaningful" word, he may still know only a handful of words. There comes a stage, however, when acquisition of vocabulary is amazingly rapid; this seems to occur when in his cognitive development the child has reached the point of perceiving that things, events, and properties have "names." During this "naming stage" he learns to ask questions like "What's that?" "What's that called?" "What does that mean?" By the time the child reaches school, say by age six, his vocabulary is often quite impressive, particularly if he has had rich verbal experiences in his environment. One estimate of average Grade I vocabulary, 23,700 words, is demonstrably faulty, but the number of different morphemes known by a first grade child could easily reach 7,500.

The manner in which a child learns the grammar of his language is still very poorly understood. In effect, the child has to perform the feat of making a kind of unconscious linguistic analysis of the language he hears, trying various patterns until he finds the patterns that are accepted and understood by his wards and that get him what he wants. That even at a fairly early age he produces incorrect analogical formations like *taked* instead of *took* demonstrates his capacity to respond to patterning in language. After the child learns to say single words (which function grammatically as if they were complete sentences), at about 20 months he begins to use simple two-word constructions in a kind of "grammar" of his own.

Here, for example, are some two-word sentences recorded from the utterances of a boy during the period 19–22 months: [1]

[1] M. D. S. Braine. *Language,* 1963, 39, 1–13.

see boy	my mommy	nightnight office	allgone shoe
see sock	my daddy	nightnight boat	allgone vitamins
see hot	my milk		allgone egg
		pretty boat	allgone lettuce
do it	byebye plane	pretty fan	allgone watch
push it	byebye man		
close it	byebye hot	more taxi	
buzz it		more melon	

Thus far, no study has been reported concerning when a child starts to learn the active use of transformations. He could, of course, learn the various transformations as independent constructions rather than learn them as variants of the same constructions, but it is difficult to imagine that the child would not take advantage of the transformational property of grammar.

The psychologist Roger Brown [2] has demonstrated that children learn the form-classes of words rather early. At least, by the age of about four they have learned that the construction *a niss* (where *niss* is a made-up word) denotes a "count noun," that is, something that comes in separate entities like *stones,* but that in the construction *Have you ever seen any niss?* a "mass noun" is denoted, that is, a substance like sand or water that doesn't ordinarily come in identifiable specimens. They also recognize that a gerund, *nissing,* denotes an action. Brown points out that in early stages of language development, most nouns are concrete, tangible objects while most verbs are observable physical actions. It would seem that very early in the course of language development, children form concepts of the form-classes we call nouns and verbs. (Doubtless they also form a concept of the adjectival form-class, although Brown did not include adjectives in his study.) Nevertheless, when children are asked to give word associations, their responses are not like those of adults; that is, they are unlikely to give words in the same form class as the stimulus. Perhaps this is simply because children have not learned the "idea" of the word-association task.

MEANING AS A PROBLEM FOR PSYCHOLOGY

In philosophy, where the study of meaning has had a secure and honored place for centuries, the problem of meaning is generally approached by considering the relationships that are said to hold between signs and the things to which they refer, or better, between signs, their referents, and the users of signs. In the previous chapter we pointed out that linguists are extremely cautious in their use of the notion of meaning; they are in any case more preoccupied with the expression system of a language than with the content or meaning system to which it presumably corresponds. Since this book is about the psychology of language and thought, we cannot pretend to give any satisfactory treatment of meaning from the standpoint of philosophy or linguistics. But since "meaning" is somehow contained or involved in language behavior, psychology can justifiably be expected to render an account of the concept of meaning that is valid within its own frame of reference. We shall try to suggest the outlines of such an account.

[2] R. W. Brown, *J. abnorm. soc. Psychol.,* 1957, 55, 1–5.

Some psychologists feel that psychology should try to dispense with the concept of meaning as much as possible. They feel it is dangerous to assume that there can be any "ideas," "thoughts," or "meanings" which are "expressed" by language in communication, because such things cannot be described or observed objectively. With this view we can have considerable sympathy, but on the other hand we feel that the explanation of a great many experimental and observational results would be extremely awkward unless we permit ourselves to assume that certain kinds of unobservable, "covert" mental events or responses take place. Introspection and subjects' verbal reports give valuable leads to what these covert events may be like, and under certain conditions we can even detect the occurrence of such events. In 1935, for example, Neal Miller conditioned a psychogalvanic response (PGR) to the letter T by pairing it with a mild electric shock delivered to the subject. Later, when the subject was instructed to think "4, T, 4, T . . . etc." to a series of successive stimuli, 4 to the first one, T to the second, and so on, it was possible to detect the PGR only in response to the even-numbered stimuli. If the PGR recorder had not been connected to the subject, there would have occurred a series of "mental" events that would have been completely unobserved. It is useful to assume that similar events occur in a great many situations—both in daily life and in psychological experiments, even though we usually have no ready means for detecting them. We must, however, be sure to justify the inferences we make about such covert events, usually by treating them as reduced or latent forms of responses that we can observe and control.

The proper solution to problems of "meaning" comes, we think, from the description of the ways in which human beings learn and use language signs in a speech community. We assume that anything we may want to say about meaning in the speech community *as a whole* can be accounted for by considering what is true for the individual members of the group taken in aggregate.

The word *meaning* is itself a linguistic form; we must explicate the use ("meaning") of this word at the very same time that we are explicating the concepts to which it corresponds, or the situations in which it arises. Solving the problem of meaning is essentially a bootstrap operation.

To construct a psychological theory of meaning, we can make use of several kinds of information available to psychologists: (1) observations of children learning linguistic behavior in naturalistic settings; (2) the paradigms of learning yielded by psychological theory and experimentation; (3) the results of experimentation in the teaching of linguistic behavior to human beings; and (4) experimental studies of the linguistic behavior of mature speakers of a language, that is, persons who have already acquired a system of linguistic habits based on "meaning."

Start with some simple cases. Even before he learns to speak, a baby learns to recognize a particular speech form as a sign of some stimulus or class of stimuli. The speech form may be a particular intonation contour, or it may be a sequence of segmental phonemes. In either case, the learning paradigm that seems to fit this case most directly is that of *classical conditioning,* where a conditioned stimulus (such as the sound of the word *dog*) presented simul-

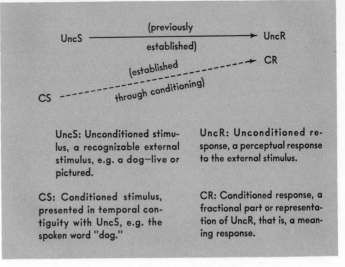

Figure 3. Establishment of a meaning response through classical conditioning. The joint presentation of UncS and CS must occur often enough to allow a reliable CR to occur.

UncS: Unconditioned stimulus, a recognizable external stimulus, e.g. a dog—live or pictured.

CS: Conditioned stimulus, presented in temporal contiguity with UncS, e.g. the spoken word "dog."

UncR: Unconditioned response, a perceptual response to the external stimulus.

CR: Conditioned response, a fractional part or representation of UncR, that is, a meaning response.

taneously with, or just before, an unconditioned stimulus (a real dog, or a picture of one), comes independently to evoke a conditioned response similar to the unconditioned response evoked by the unconditioned stimulus (see Figure 3).[3]

But what, exactly, is the unconditioned response to the sight of a dog or a picture of a dog? Some writers on this subject have tried to identify such a response with *overt* responses, such as patting, withdrawal, signs of emotion, but this line of reasoning is unnecessary and probably incorrect. It seems sufficient to say that before a child starts to learn the meanings of linguistic signs, he learns to make pure perceptual responses to objects and events in the world around him. He recognizes certain stimuli or stimulus configurations as being similar to configurations he has experienced before. Certain faces, toys, items of wearing apparel, foods, and so on, come to have perceptual identities in the child's experience; the same can be said of qualities of experience such as colors, sizes, intensities of sound, and experiences of touch, as well as experiences of motor action (such as pulling, hitting, eating). Perceptually, these experiences are of constancies; for example, a favorite doll is recognized as a constant, identifiable experience no matter from what angle it is viewed, and no matter how it is felt or touched. How such stimulus configurations can be recognized as constancies is not directly our problem here. For convenience, let us make the reasonable assumption that there are in the repertoire of young children a large number of perceptual identifying responses to common experiences. These responses are prior to, and independent of, language; deaf children have them. They are covert responses that are ordinarily unobservable, but their presence can be inferred from the overt signs of recognition that the child often makes.

This long digression was necessary to establish what kind of responses function as the unconditioned responses when an infant is conditioned to

[3] For information on classical conditioning and other basic learning concepts applied in this chapter, see S. A. Mednick. *Learning.* Englewood Cliffs, N.J.: Prentice-Hall, 1964, a volume in the Foundations of Modern Psychology Series.

respond to a linguistic sign by classical conditioning.[4] But it is well known that the conditioned response is seldom precisely the same as the unconditioned response. So it is in the learning of a response to a language sign. When a child becomes conditioned to respond to a linguistic sign such as "dog," he does not have the full unconditioned response; he does not hallucinate the sight of a dog! Rather, the conditioned response is some fractional representation of the identifying response to dogs, or to particular dogs. Or more generally, it is a fractional representation of the identifying response to whatever perceptual invariant is involved in the linguistic sign. Many psychologists call it a *mediating response,* because it can become a stimulus for further behavior.

Thus, in a simple case, "understanding" of a linguistic sign occurs when it evokes the conditioned response related to the unconditioned response that would be evoked by the stimulus or stimulus configuration which this sign "represents." This conditioned response may be called a "meaning response." Both unconditioned and conditioned responses here may be covert and inaccessible to external observation by any ordinary means. From the standpoint of the hearer, the "meaning" of a linguistic form is the conditioned response it evokes. Even in the early stages of language learning, this meaning may be quite complex and may contain both denotative and connotative components (these terms are discussed below). It may be partially "incorrect" from the standpoint of adult language. But learning the "correct" meanings of linguistic signs may be as much a matter of sharpening and revising perceptions as of learning anything about the signs. Learning that "dog" does not apply to horses is partly a matter of refining the perceptual responses involved in each case.

Parenthetically, it should be noted that linguistic signs themselves are stimuli which the child has to learn to recognize as perceptual constancies, just as he has to learn to recognize other kinds of stimuli. A word has to be recognized no matter who says it, or how. Also, linguistic signs themselves have certain perceptual qualities (for example, the smoothness of an *m* sound or the shrillness of a sibilant) that become associated, even if only very marginally and peripherally, with meaning responses; this fact may account for some of the findings of "phonetic symbolism" (pp. 6–7).

So far we have talked only about meaning responses in the *hearer* of language. We must also account for the behavior of the speaker who utters the linguistic signs to which the child responds, and also for his learning of signs when he was first learning language.

Since speech is a motor response, the learning model that seems most appropriate for explaining it is the *operant* paradigm; an operant response is one whose strength is a function of the degree to which it has been followed by rewards (positive reinforcements). In the case of speech, the reinforcement is always *social,* for it is provided by other persons in the individual's environment. B. F. Skinner[5] has drawn attention to several ways in which a speech response may arise. It may be learned as an *echoic* response, that is,

---

[4] It will be noticed that in this account we assume that the perceptual response is an involuntary type of response similar to those of the autonomic system, and therefore subject to classical conditioning. See Mednick, *ibid.,* pp. 52–53 for a comparison of operant and classical conditioning.

[5] B. F. Skinner. *Verbal behavior.* New York: Appleton-Century-Crofts, 1957.

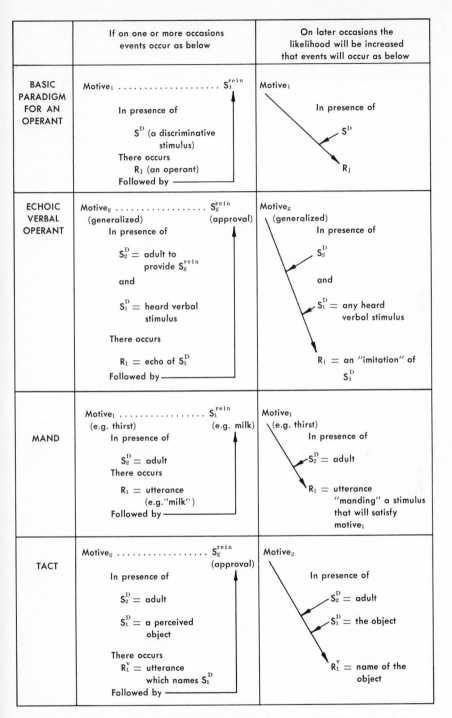

Figure 4. Operant paradigms for the learning and maintenance of verbal responses.

as an imitation of a heard stimulus which the parent, say, may reward if it is sufficiently similar to the stimulus. Or it may be learned as a *mand*—as a response which starts out as a random speech utterance but which is adequate to cause the parent to provide a stimulus that happens to satisfy some current need of the child. For example, a parent might take a random utterance on the part of the child as sufficiently close to *ball* to make him think the child is asking for (*manding*) a ball, whereupon it is given to the child, thus satisfying the desire that (one may suppose) he happens to have for the ball. Such a sequence, repeated several times, may enhance the probability that *ball* or something like it will be uttered by the child whenever he wants a ball. Still another way in which a verbal response can be acquired, according to Skinner's notions, is as a *tact*. A child who for any reason makes a particular verbal response in the presence of (in con*tact* with) a given objective stimulus, and is rewarded for doing so, may learn to make this response, or some variant of it, whenever he experiences the relevant stimulus.

It will be noted that we have said nothing about "meaning" in this account. Skinner's formulations concern only the objective relationships between certain stimuli and certain responses; in his view, the "meanings" of the linguistic forms that happen to be involved in verbal responses can be completely accounted for by stating the contingencies under which the verbal responses occur.

Skinner's paradigms can be demonstrated experimentally; in fact, they are matters of common observation. With the *mand* paradigm one can train a child to make a certain verbal response whenever he has a particular need; and with the *tact* paradigm one could readily train a child to name something with any arbitrary verbal response one might like. The only difficulty that might be encountered in either of these cases is that one might have to wait a long time before the desired response occurs, to give one the opportunity to reward it in an appropriate stimulus context. This difficulty can be avoided by first teaching the child to make echoic responses, and then chaining mands and tacts to these. At a later stage of the child's development, he could be taught to make *texting* responses (that is, verbal responses to printed or written text stimuli) as discriminative operants, and these in turn could be chained with mands, tacts, and other kinds of verbal responses. One could thus in theory build up a quite elaborate system of verbal responses in the child. In fact, this formulation underlies the "programed instruction" or "teaching machine" movement.

Compelling as Skinner's formulations may be, they present certain theoretical difficulties, and not all psychologists are satisfied with the solutions that Skinner has proposed. The theory as a whole banks heavily on the concept of reinforcement, but not everyone is willing to accept the proposition that reinforcement is the crucial factor in learning.[6] Also, the theory cannot easily account for the fact that a language response learned in one way generally is immediately available for use in other ways. A child who has learned to understand a word (through classical conditioning) may later use it as a mand (that is, a means of satisfying some need) or as a tact (that

---

[6] This matter is discussed at length in the book in this series about learning, by Mednick, already cited.

is, as a name of some object or event) without going through the particular behavioral processes theoretically required in learning mands or tacts. It seems desirable to postulate behavioral links among these different processes; after all, they all occur in the same organism—an organism complex enough, surely, to allow for such links.

If we look again, more closely, at the paradigms postulated by Skinner, we notice that in all cases there must be covert perceptual responses to the rewards (in the case of mands) or to the discriminative stimuli (in the case of tacts). In the process of operant conditioning, then, classical conditioning, or something very much like it, must be going on in parallel. That is to say, a response that we may regard as a "meaning response" is conditioned to the reinforcement (in the case of a mand) or to the discriminative stimulus (in the case of a tact). Since the meaning response is a conditioned, covert perceptual response to a linguistic sign, whether it arises in learning to speak or to comprehend language, once learned it can function in any of these contexts, and this fact would account for the transfer that takes place from one behavioral context to another.

So far we have arrived at the conclusion that in the early stages of language learning, "meaning" arises from the fact that many linguistic forms evoke conditioned, covert perceptual responses. Eventually, a child becomes

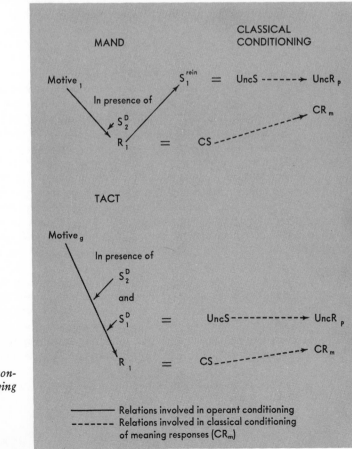

Figure 5. Classical conditioning accompanying mands and tacts.

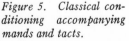

aware of or generalizes this meaning relationship; as *he* perceives it, meaning is a direct correspondence between words, on the one hand, and objects, events, qualities, and other states of affairs in the world of his experience.[7] This perception occurs in what we have called the "naming stage" when the child becomes aware that objects have names and that the meanings of unfamiliar words can be explained to him. Thus, he arrives at a *concept* of the word *meaning;* that is, he learns how to use expressions like *meaning* and *to mean something.*

For the psychologist, however, the meaning relationship lies wholly in behavior. It is a relationship between experiences that we call "language signs" and other experiences that may be called "meaning responses" or "mediating responses" that are gathered together or organized into "concepts."

We are now ready to sketch how this account of meaning deals with several issues concerning meaning that are of particular importance in psychology.

Denotative Meaning

In all the paradigms of verbal learning we have presented, the child gradually learns what range of situations yields the highest probability of social reinforcement. That is, through processes of discrimination learning and stimulus generalization, a child learns what properties or patterns of stimulation are critical for social reinforcement when he utters a given linguistic form. For example, he learns what characteristics an animal has in order for it to be called a "dog." To the extent that this learning on the part of the child corresponds to comparable processes of learning on the part of other members of the speech community, we may say that the child has learned the denotative meaning of the form in the speech community. We can describe the denotative meaning of a form by specifying the properties or patterns of stimulation which are essential—that is, *criterial*—for its socially approved use in the speech community. Dictionary definitions are successful to the extent that they can do this.

In theory, this analysis can apply to every item in a linguistic expression system—that is, not only to the words that are names of objects, events, and attributes in the physical and biological environment, but also to the words that name abstractions and relationships, and to words, forms, and constructions that have a purely grammatical function. Sometimes the patterns of stimulation that are criterial for the use of grammatical elements are solely verbal, for example, the grammatical context that evokes the use of the infinitive marker *to.*

As the uses of words and other elements of a linguistic expression system are being learned, a corresponding development of implicit mediating responses takes place. This probably occurs by virtue of the paradigms of classical conditioning of perceptual responses that we have given. The perceptual constancies, or invariants, that the child acquires preverbally are to some extent modified and re-sorted along the lines dictated by the referential

---

[7] In her autobiography, Helen Keller describes vividly how as a deaf-blind child she first became aware of this relationship.

patterns of the language symbols he learns. The denotative meaning of a linguistic form is reflected in a "concept"—a bundle of implicit mediating responses which are linked with the properties and patterns of stimulation that are criterial for that form in the speech community.

Connotative Meaning

As an individual accumulates experience with the patterns of stimulation corresponding to a given linguistic form, he responds not only to the criterial attributes of these patterns but also to the noncriterial attributes—attributes that occur with these patterns in either external or verbal contexts with considerable regularity but do not govern reinforcement by the speech community. For example, "likeableness" may be a frequent attribute of "dogs," but it is irrelevant to the denotation of the word *dog*. An individual's responses to noncriterial attributes become attached, through conditioning processes, to the meaning responses or concepts evoked by a linguistic form. That part of the meaning response which does not correspond to criterial attributes may be called the *connotative meaning* of a form. Fundamentally, connotative meaning is an individual matter because it depends on the experiences that an individual has happened to have. Since the experiences of individuals in a speech community are in general rather similar, there are many similarities among the connotative meanings they have. But to the extent that people's experiences and attitudes differ, connotative meanings can also differ. Even on the assumption that people agree on the denotation of a word like *Democrat,* we still cannot say that they will agree widely on its connotation. In Chapter 7 we describe some methods for studying the connotations of linguistic symbols and the concepts to which they correspond.

Meaningfulness

The concept, or meaning response, associated with a word experienced in a wide variety of contexts will expand in the extent of its connotative meaning, and this richness of connotation may be called "meaningfulness." One way of measuring meaningfulness, due to C. E. Noble, is based on the rate at which subjects give verbal associations to a word. Words of very rare or limited use or nonsense syllables are found to have low degrees of meaningfulness, although it is difficult to find nonsense syllables that are completely devoid of meaningfulness by this measure.

Situational Meaning

The problem posed here is this: What is the "meaning" of a sentence uttered in a particular situation, and how is it related to the meanings of the linguistic forms and constructions that compose it? A sentence can be likened to a computer program; in fact, that is precisely what it is: a set of directions for the human thinking machine. The hearer or the reader of a sentence constructs its meaning by following the "directions" it provides in terms of the concepts and conceptual relationships it evokes, also utilizing whatever further information he may have concerning the situation in which he hears it. This process may be called *interpretation*. A string of linguistic signs that cannot be interpreted, like "words straighten poverty without every encounter," is devoid of situational meaning.

Intention vs. Meaning

If a sentence is like a program for a thinking machine, it is also an artifact created by the speaker. The speaker's intention in creating a sentence is not necessarily correlated with the situational meaning the sentence has for the hearer. The speaker may not be fully successful in creating a sentence that will be interpreted as he intends it to be, or he may be only too successful in creating a sentence that he knows will be interpreted in a way that will deceive the hearer.

SECOND-LANGUAGE LEARNING AND BILINGUALISM

There are cases when the environment of a child contains more than one language—as when each parent speaks a different language, or when the child is reared in a bilingual community. In the early years of childhood, such children can often learn more than one language with ease. The circumstances of learning are like those of a mother tongue in each case. Sometimes there are interferences, of course: Occasionally responses from one language system will intrude into speech in the other language. It appears that learning is most successful when the situations in which the two languages are learned are kept as distinct as possible: For example, the child learns one language from one parent, the other language from the other parent. This conclusion is in accord with the theoretical proposition that the cues for competing responses should be kept as distinct as possible. Resulting from such a learning situation is what may be called *coordinate* bilingualism, because the two language systems tend to be parallel and independent of each other, with independent sets of meaning responses. There is no good evidence that such bilingualism retards mental development; most instances where retardation has been reported can be explained as the result of attempting to teach the child in a language he has not learned adequately.

Past the age of early childhood, it appears to be much more difficult for an individual to learn a second language system coordinate to a well-learned first language. Typically, a person learns a second language partly in terms of the kinds of meanings already learned in the first language. In this type of bilingualism, called *compound* bilingualism, second-language responses are grafted on to the first-language responses, and both are made to a common set of meaning responses. Other things being equal, the compound bilingual is less fluent in the second language, and the kinds of expressions he uses in the second language bear tell-tale traces of the structure of the first language.

Efficient methods of teaching second languages attempt to duplicate certain features of the learning situation that produces coordinate bilingualism—maximizing the degree to which new language responses are made to objective, nonverbal situations or to contexts utilizing previously acquired responses in the new language, and minimizing the use of the native tongue except where greater efficiency in teaching is attained by using it to explain meaning and grammatical points. In view of the large number of new habits that must be made as highly automatic as possible, successful second-language learning requires a considerable investment of time, a major proportion of which must be spent in repetitive drill. Audiovisual devices, such as tape recorders and teaching machines, can be of considerable assistance in language learning. Sometimes language teachers overlook the importance of conducting drill in accordance with principles of learning. For example, drill is probably of little use unless there is more or less constant feedback of information to the learner concerning the degree to which he is approximating the desired responses.

According to widespread opinion, many of the difficulties the learner has with the phonology, vocabulary, and grammar of the second language are due to the interference of habits from the first language. To some extent this may be true, but it has also been reported that with very careful shaping of new responses by a proper schedule of reinforcement, the problem of interference is considerably reduced.

In thinking about the learning and teaching of second languages, we may find it useful to refer to some distinctions made by the anthropologist E. T. Hall.[8] When conducted in a school situation, second-language learning tends to be largely what Hall calls *formal* learning—learning guided by conscious, deliberate effort on the part of the learner; there is also considerable infusion of what he calls *technical* learning—learning guided by the application of rules and logic. Very little of it is similar to the kind of *informal* learning—which takes place "out of the learner's awareness"—that occurs in much early first-language learning. Although formal and technical learning may have some place in second-language learning, it is probable that a faster, more appropriate kind of learning can be attained by shifting the balance in favor of "informal" learning.

[8] E. T. Hall. *The silent language*. New York: Doubleday, 1959.

Aspects
of Language Behavior

Now that we have studied the nature of language as a sign system (Chapter 2) and the basic principles involved in the learning of language (Chapter 3), we are ready to go into some detail on how language behavior actually takes place. The bulk of this chapter will be concerned with the production and understanding of speech—in both physiological and psychological aspects. Here we will find it useful to consider language behavior from a statistical point of view. The latter part of the chapter, however, will consider the application of the psychology of language to reading.

44

4

The neurological processes involved in speech are extremely complex. Not only must all the muscles controlling the speech mechanism be precisely coordinated in order to produce acceptable sounds, but also the utterance must be composed and arranged in such a way as to be meaningful. Here we shall discuss only a few important generalizations from scientific studies of the neurophysiology of the speech apparatus.

It is generally agreed that speech functions take place in only one hemisphere of the brain, usually the side of the brain opposite to hand preference; thus, the left hemisphere is the "dominant hemisphere" of most right-handed people. In doubtful cases medical specialists can determine laterality by noting which side affects speech when sodium amytal is injected into one of the arteries supplying blood to the brain. There are cases on record of complete hemispherectomy; if the hemisphere excised controls speech, the patient will not be able to learn or relearn language unless he is still quite young (no more than 10 years of age, say).

Beyond this, brain physiologists either cannot agree on the precise function of the several cortical areas, or feel the evidence is insufficient to allow any definite conclusions. In the nineteenth century, Paul Broca's discovery (1861) of a "speech area" in the left temporal lobe, along with various other observations of the speech difficulties of individuals with identifiable brain lesions, held out the hope that it might be possible to assign specific language functions to particular regions in the brain, and a number of such areas were marked out. Careful sifting of the evidence accumulated since then, however, does not support any such simple account. For example, when a lesion occurs in a certain brain region, accompanied by a particular behavior symptom, it is impossible to ascertain what the function of that brain region is, because it may be either an area that originates some kind of neural impulse, or one that integrates and transmits impulses received from another area. Further, brain lesions are seldom well localized; often they are the scattered areas served by a dysfunctioning blood vessel. On the other hand, Wilder Penfield's technique of observing patients' speech reactions during stimulation of the surgically exposed cortex promises to enable us to assign functions of speech behavior to specific areas of the cortex (see Figure 6).

We can make certain inferences about the neural control of speech production from the phenomena caused by delayed auditory feedback. These rather astounding effects were discovered with the introduction of the tape recorder. When equipment is specially arranged so that whatever a person says is fed back to his ears through headphones, not instantaneously, as in normal speech, but with a short time lag of up to one second, his speech shows certain kinds of disturbances—changes in rate, intensity, and temporal pattern—that sometimes sound like a bad case of stuttering. The effects are most pronounced if the time-delay is about one-fifth of a second. Although there are individual differences in the ability to resist them, every normal-hearing person shows some effects. The phenomenon suggests that normal speech in-

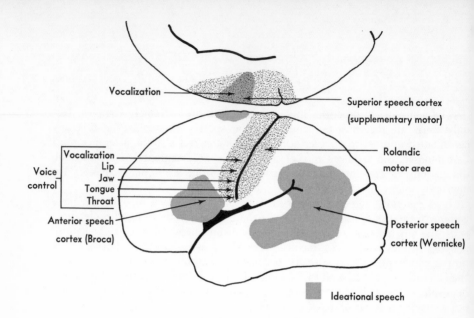

Figure 6. Speech areas in the dominant hemisphere (side view, below; medial section, above), after W. Penfield and L. Roberts. According to these authors, three areas, as shown, are devoted to the ideational elaboration of speech, and two areas to its vocalization. (Adapted from Speech and brain mechanisms *by Penfield and Roberts, by permission of Princeton University Press, copyright 1959.)*

volves a perceptual self-monitoring process which is interfered with by the delayed feedback.

SOME ASPECTS OF TALKING

Speech in ordinary discourse occurs at various rates depending on the situation and the characteristics of speakers. The situation evokes speech partly as a function of the extent to which the individual has been reinforced or rewarded in similar situations. For example, William Verplanck has shown [1] that people are more likely to continue a conversation if their interlocutors agree with them than if they disagree with them; at least, for the people used in Verplanck's study, agreement was apparently more reinforcing than disagreement. (In reinforcement theory, a stimulus that enhances the probability of a response is *defined* as a reinforcer.) A previous history of reinforcement or nonreinforcement is one possible explanation for the large individual differences in the degree to which people participate in discussions, ask questions in class, or tell jokes.

An even more basic trait is a person's characteristic speech rate when he is well motivated to talk, a rate that varies widely from individual to individual. It is not so much a function of the rate at which a person speaks the

[1] W. S. Verplanck. *J. abnorm. soc. Psychol.,* 1955, 51, 668–676.

words themselves, as of the degree to which he interrupts the flow of his speech with pauses and hesitation signs like [ah, ər, əm]. Frieda Goldman-Eisler has demonstrated consistency within the individual: For the slower speakers, the momentary "bursts" of rapid talking usually occur with highly redundant, automatized utterances, giving way to slower speech when the content is more involved and less redundant.[2]

Most people, if not all, exhibit hesitation phenomena in their speech, with either filled pauses containing sounds like those mentioned above, or simple unfilled pauses, that is, silences. Here again, there are wide individual differences; some people have trained themselves to avoid at least filled pauses. There is some evidence that these two types of pauses have different functions in speech. Unfilled pauses result from thinking to formulate ideas; filled pauses are more likely to reflect anxiety. Study and observation of these hesitation phenomena can have two uses; first, they are presumably reflections of psychological processes in the construction of sentences, and second, they can be shown to have significance for the clinical psychologist. In fact, any deviation of spontaneous speech from what a simple reading of an edited transcript would be can conceivably have some psychological significance, and this includes all the various kinds of false starting and backtracking, voice quavers and tremors, and abnormal stress and intonation patterns that a trained linguist might detect in a highly detailed phonetic transcription of an utterance. A number of clinical psychologists have found these phenomena useful in identifying sources of anxiety and conflict in patients undergoing therapeutic interviews.

THE CONSTRUCTION OF UTTERANCES

How does a speaker who has learned his native language well construct utterances? Our discussion will revolve around the speaker, because we can assume that a writer merely writes down, very deliberately and perhaps in highly edited form, the sentences he imagines he would say as a speaker. The differences between spoken and written language are for the most part obvious and need not be commented upon here.

For the purposes of a scientific discussion, we have to make the assumption that everything a speaker may say is completely determined, that is, dependent on antecedent conditions. The causal relations may often be very complex; indeed, we have to speak of *multiple* causation, because any act of speech may be affected by a large number of antecedent conditions operating simultaneously. It is our task to establish generalizations concerning the way antecedent conditions affect a given kind of event. It is often surprising how satisfactorily a given speech act can be accounted for *retrospectively*. For example, in a classic article on "the psychology of invention in a simple case," the educational psychologist Thorndike [3] asked students to guess or make up the meanings of rare or nonsense words like *amerce, besom,* and *debrag.* Even though most of the responses to any given stimulus were

---

[2] F. Goldman-Eisler. *Brit. J. Psychol.,* 1951, 42, 355–362; 1954, 45, 94–107.
[3] E. L. Thorndike. *Psychol. Rev.,* 1949, 56, 192–199.

different, Thorndike believed he could give plausible reasons for the guesses. One student, for instance, defined *amerce* as "to duck under water," obviously influenced by the word *immerse.*

A retrospective account, of course, is not a satisfactory demonstration of the power of scientific generalizations; we can validate our generalizations better if we show that we can predict future events with a high degree of success. To what extent can we do this in the case of language?

Word Association Studies

One of the most extensively studied kinds of verbal behavior is what is called *free association.* (We didn't say "thoroughly studied," for there are still plenty of problems in it to challenge the researcher.) The standard technique is to present a subject with a number of words (usually printed) and ask him to respond to each word, orally or in writing, with "the first word that comes to mind." Various kinds of stimuli can be presented, but, chiefly through force of tradition, most of the research has been based on the Kent-Rosanoff (K-R) list, named after two psychologists who developed it in 1910 as a device for eliciting verbal responses that might reveal personality, motivation, and affect. (The list is seldom used for that purpose now.) It consists of 100 nouns and adjectives, a few of which can also be taken as verbs. The free association task is admittedly not highly similar to anything that occurs in normal everyday behavior, but it serves as a relatively simple, circumscribed setting for laboratory studies of verbal responses.

Here we are chiefly interested in how well we can predict an individual's response to a word. Even without knowing much about him except that he is a native speaker of English, our predictions will be reasonably good—very good in the case of some words, for lists have been drawn up of the more common responses to the K-R lists in large representative samples of adolescents and adults. In one such listing,[4] over the whole K-R list, the most common, or "primary," responses accounted for 37.5 per cent of all the responses; the second most common responses accounted for 13.7 per cent of the total; and the third most common accounted for 8.0 per cent; in all, the three most common responses accounted for 59.1 per cent of all the responses.

These figures represent a degree of prediction that would be highly satisfactory in other contexts, say, predicting the weather. But they can be made even better by taking account of certain characteristics of the respondents. For example, the age of the respondent makes a considerable difference. Whereas adolescents and adults tend to give what have been called paradigmatic responses (that is, responses that are of the same part of speech as the stimulus), children tend to give syntagmatic responses, that is, responses that might naturally follow the word in a sentence: for example, *BRIGHT— sun.* It has been claimed that this result means that children do not have their language responses organized into form classes as well as adults do, but it may also mean, as suggested on page 33, that children have a different concept of the task of giving "the first word that comes to mind." That is,

[4] W. A. Russell and J. J. Jenkins. *The complete Minnesota norms for responses to 100 words from the Kent-Rosanoff word association test.* University of Minnesota Department of Psychology, 1954.

the kind of set with which the task is approached may be an important determinant of response.

The role of set is seen, for example, in the consistent individual differences [5] among people of college age in the tendency to respond with words that are opposites (antonyms) of the stimulus words, or with words whose meaning contrasts in some way with that of the stimulus word (for instance, *moth* as a response to *BUTTERFLY*). Some people give such responses on almost every occasion; others rarely do. Therefore, if we can make a prior determination of an individual's tendency to make this class of response, we can predict particular responses to the K-R test with even more accuracy than we can from the general population statistics.

Of course, it is also possible to arrange cues that have a high probability of triggering specific responses. One way of doing this is to give the first letter of the response desired, and the number of letters in it. Try these stimuli:

BIRD .....   F — —
UGLY .....   D — — — — — —

Another way is to give the stimulus word only after several other words have been presented. Davis Howes and Charles Osgood found that whereas the normal percentage of *hell* as a response to *DARK* was very small, it rose markedly when the word was given in the context of the words *devil—fearful—sinister*.

All these experiments tell us something about the organization of verbal response repertoires in those who have learned a language well—namely, that when the context arouses a certain set, a given stimulus has a high probability of evoking one of a small number of responses that can be specified in advance. The greater the number of background context factors, the more highly determined (that is, predictable) is the response. We could expect this generalization to apply not only to responses in a free association test but also to verbal behavior in general.

Having persuaded ourselves that speech behavior can be treated scientifically in a deterministic system, we can now inquire into the possible stimulus-response patterns that operate in a normal speech situation. To make the problem concrete, let's consider the antecedents of the following utterance:

"It's getting stuffy in here; would you mind opening the window?"

You can easily imagine the situation in which this utterance might occur. The first part might be called an observation concerning the situation; the second part, a request. Look at the first part. In form, it is a predication about *it;* but notice that in English we have a large class of utterances beginning with *it* and making observations about general conditions: the weather (*it's warm today*), the time (*it's Tuesday; it's late; it's five o'clock*). Linguistically, perhaps, we might say that *it* is a substitute for *the weather, the atmosphere, the day,* or *the time.* But there are certain expressions where any substitute for *it* would be extremely awkward and rare. For

[5] J. B. Carroll, P. M. Kjeldergaard, and A. S. Carton. *J. verb. Learning verb. Behav.,* 1962–63, 1, 22–30.

example, *It's the first week of July* would hardly be said as *The week is the first one in July*. Furthermore, normally the pronoun *it* is used only as a substitute for some previously named nominal, or as a "temporary subject" (as in the sentence to follow). It seems reasonable to assume that the construction *It* + (predication about time or weather) is a highly predictable response to any situation in which the speaker has occasion to comment on time, weather, or other general environmental circumstances; that is, it is a response that is learned as a separate and distinct unit.

The formulation of an utterance *It's getting stuffy in here* is normally very rapid; perhaps it is gratuitous to think that the speaker's performance can be dissected into a series of decisions made in sequence. Nevertheless, hesitations where the speaker seems to search for the right word (as in *It's getting— er, well, stuffy in here*), suggest that selection takes place on two levels; first, on a grammatical level (selection of a construction or a transformation of one, including the selection of form classes), and second, on a lexical level (selection of particular words, in appropriate form classes, to fit in the constructions). Thus, having selected the construction *it* + (predication about time or weather) the speaker proceeds to fill in his construction. But this construction in turn demands another construction, namely, some form of predication; the form selected (linking verb + adjectival) is presumably a response to an experienced quality (the atmosphere). Other components of the situation —current time, perceptible change in conditions or the immediate surrounding environment, and place—dictate filling in this nest of constructions in such a way as to produce the utterance *It's getting stuffy in here*.

It is worth noting that a declarative construction was selected as the form for the sentence as a whole. The speaker might have said *Isn't it getting stuffy in here?* or *How stuffy it's getting in here!* Linguistically, these are both transformations of the basic declarative construction. An interesting question is this: If one of these transformations had been used, is there some sense in which it was psychologically a transformation? That is, was there some process by which the finished utterance was derived from a "kernel" declarative sentence? [6] We cannot currently answer this question. George Miller has developed evidence suggesting that the speed with which people can make or find transformations of sentences presented to them is related to the number and order of transformations that are involved in the process, but this says nothing about how sentences are formulated in the first place.[7] A person could learn to formulate nonkernel sentences as easily as kernel sentences.

For example, the second part of the hypothetical utterance cited above is linguistically a request in the form of a yes-no transformation of *You would mind opening the window*. But there is little reason to suppose that the speaker formulates the utterance as a kernel and then transforms it. The actual unit of selection may, in fact, be a construction already transformed. In the present case, *Would you mind* . . . is such a frequent way of formulating a polite request that it may well be, idiom-like, learned as a distinct unit; that it conforms to a certain linguistic pattern is psychologically of no more

[6] See p. 25.
[7] G. A. Miller. *Amer. Psychologist,* 1962, 17, 748–762.

interest than the fact that an idiom like *Mark you well* deviates from the normal pattern for the imperative transformation. Exactly what is a selection unit in the behavior of an individual depends on his behavioral history, and only secondarily on linguistic units. Many whole utterances are learned as units, sometimes with little meaning, or incorrectly as in the case of a child in the first grade who thought the flag salute began *I pledge a legion to the flag*. Most of the available studies of verbal behavior that we can report—studies of free association, controlled association, naming behavior, categorizing behavior, and so on—have more to say about the selection of lexical units, or "content" words, than about the selection of grammatical constructions, and thus what we have said here about selection processes is largely speculative.

If we refer to the list of basic expression-types in Chapter 2 (p. 24), we see that at the highest level of utterance formulation, the "choice" is between four kinds of nonsentential expressions or two kinds of sentence-types. It would not be difficult to specify the situations that evoke each of the four nonsentential expressions (greetings, calls, exclamatories, and responses to another speaker).

The basic situation evoking a sentence-type (as distinguished from a non-sentential expression) is one in which "information" concerning some stimulus—either objective or subjective—is handled. If the sheer existence of the stimulus is in question, the situation calls for use of an existence-assertion sentence type; if some perceived attribute of the stimulus is in question, selection of some form of predication occurs, the exact form depending on the kind of attribute involved. For example, an attribute perceived as a "variable quality" becomes a predication with a linking verb and an adjective construction; a large class of other perceptions is encoded into predications with an intransitive or transitive verb.

Likewise, the situations evoking certain transformed constructions can be specified and experimentally verified. The writer, for example, has studied the elicitations of statements, questions, and imperatives in a miniature two-person game situation. As might be expected, an utterance will normally be in declarative form (the null transformation) if the speaker perceives his information to be greater than that of his hearer; it is likely to be in the form of a question if he perceives his information to be less than that of his hearer. It can be in imperative form if he desires his hearer to perform an action or do something to arrive at some particular state of affairs, but social amenities permit the unadorned imperative only when the action is for the hearer's own benefit (*Drink some water*); otherwise the imperative (*Give me some water*) is either supplemented with the expression *Please* or is replaced by questions (*Will you give me a glass of water?*) or statements (*I'd like some water*).

Experimental results have also suggested that the choice of what element in a situation is to be the subject of a sentence is an important determinant of whether the active or passive voice will be used. In reporting a baseball game we might say "Jones hit Smith with a fast ball" if we are primarily interested in what Jones did, but we would be likely to say "Smith was hit with a fast ball" if we are detailing what happened to Smith and why he was sent to the hospital.

Victor Yngve [8] has developed a model of language structure which suggests some of the processes whereby we produce sentences. He assumes that all rewrite rules (p. 20) in a grammar are binary, that is, that no construction can be expanded into more than two other constructions. For example, a noun phrase construction can be expanded into another noun phrase and a prepositional modifier construction, as in *pictures → pictures + of Rome*. The process of producing a sentence, according to Yngve, is one of successively expanding constructions until every construction is either expanded into two other constructions, or filled in with words. Since uttering a sentence is a temporal matter, the "left-hand" parts of any construction must be expanded before the right-hand parts. Yngve observes that we tend to avoid making too many successive expansions of left-hand parts of constructions, because every time we do, the utterance (and, perhaps, the expansion) of the right-hand parts is that much more delayed and less likely to be remembered. The phrase *very much more clearly projected pictures of Rome* (diagrammed in Figure 7) contains five successive left-hand expansions and one right-hand expansion. Yngve suggests that the number of nested left-handed expansions (which he calls the "depth" of a sentence's grammar) is generally limited by human memory storage capacity. His hypothesis is that depth seldom exceeds the "magic number 7 ± 2" that George Miller has pointed to as the measure of human memory storage capacity. The transformations noted by other grammarians are in Yngve's view mainly useful in enabling us to avoid excessive grammatical depth. For example, instead of saying "What what what he wanted cost in New York would buy in Germany amazed us" (as we would have to say using only active verbs) we can say "We were amazed by what could be bought in Germany for the cost in New York of what he wanted."

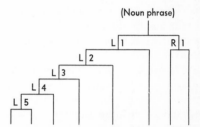

(Noun phrase)

very much more clearly projected pictures of Rome

Figure 7. Left-hand (L) and right-hand (R) expansions of a phrase.

LANGUAGE BEHAVIOR FROM A STATISTICAL POINT OF VIEW

Tabulations of the frequency of occurrence of phonemes, letters, words, and other language units are of practical usefulness in such enterprises as developing teaching materials, designing systems of stenography, and breaking secret codes. These tabulations have also been of interest to psychologists and others interested in language behavior, and they are particularly useful in studying speech production and reception.

[8] V. Yngve. *Scientific American,* June 1962, 206 (6), 68–76.

G. K. Zipf some years ago noticed that in English and several other languages there was a rather close relation between word frequency and word length and interpreted this as evidence of a natural law of efficiency in language structure: Imagine how inefficient it would be to write or speak a language in which all the common words were long and the rare ones short (if, indeed, there could be sufficient variety in short, rare words). Zipf also

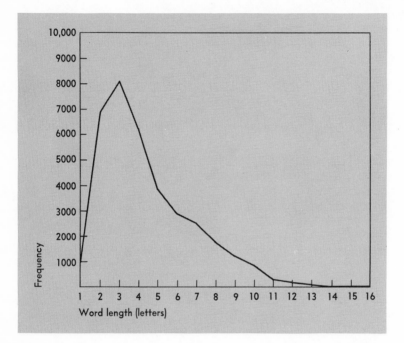

Figure 8.   The relation between word length and word frequency (in terms of word tokens occurring in typical samples of text). (Data from G. A. Miller, E. B. Newman, and E. A. Friedman. Inform. and control, *1958, 1, 370–389.)*

noticed an even more interesting relationship—what he called the rank-frequency law. If you take a compilation of the frequencies of words in large samples of English, such as the well-known Thorndike-Lorge count,[9] arrange the words in order of frequency, and then plot the logarithm of the word frequency against the logarithm of the rank of the word in frequency, you will usually get an almost perfect straight line with a negative slope of 45°. Mathematically, this implies that frequency times rank will yield a constant value for the whole frequency range in a given sample. Zipf believed that deviations from this straight-line relationship, as might be found in samples of the speech of children or of schizophrenics, are valuable indicators of

[9] E. L. Thorndike and I. Lorge. *The teacher's word book of 30,000 words.* New York: Teachers College, Columbia University, 1944.

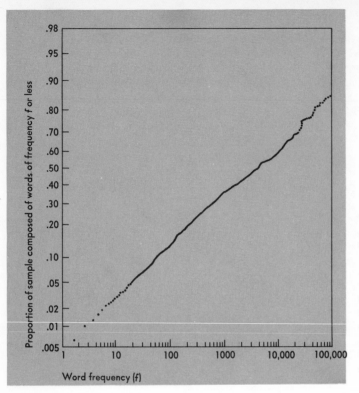

Figure 9. Cumulative word-frequency distribution for the Lorge Magazine Count (4.5 million words), plotted on logarithmic-normal coordinates. (Adapted from data of D. Howes. In J. Money (ed.). Reading disability. Baltimore: Johns Hopkins Press, 1962.)

developmental or other abnormalities in language behavior. Davis Howes [10] has elegantly demonstrated that this is true for the speech of aphasics, although he believes the word-frequency distribution is better described as a logarithmic normal distribution (see Figure 9).

The word-frequency distribution, however it is analyzed, reflects a relationship between the number of types (different words) in a sample and the number of tokens (total words). (The terms *type* and *token* were introduced in Chapter 1, page 2.) Sometimes the type-token ratio (the number of different words divided by the number of total words) is used as a measure of the diversity or richness of vocabulary in a sample, but it should be noted that this ratio will tend to decrease as sample size increases, other things being equal, because fewer and fewer of the words will *not* have occurred in the samples already counted. A measure of vocabulary diversity that is approximately independent of sample size is the number of different words divided by the square root of twice the number of words in the sample.

The development of a mathematical theory of information transmission by Claude Shannon, a communications engineer, has enabled psychologists to gain new perspectives on statistical studies of language behavior.[11] The

[10] Davis Howes. A quantitative approach to word blindness. In John Money. *Reading disability.* Baltimore: Johns Hopkins Press, 1962, p. 135.

[11] C. Shannon and W. Weaver. *The mathematical theory of communication.* Urbana: University of Illinois Press, 1949.

key idea is a method of measuring the "information" contained in a message. "Information" is used here in a special sense—it really means "the informativeness of the symbols in a message relative to one's expectations of those symbols." Here are three ten-letter "messages," in each of which the last letter has been deleted; try to guess what letter has been deleted: AAAAAAAAA-; PRRNWBITK-; GENERATIO-. For the first one, probably you will guess that the deleted letter is A, and if indeed the tenth letter is A it will not be very informative for you. In fact, if the tenth letter is something *other* than A, say F, it will probably strike you as very informative. Since the second message is a random sequence of letters, you would have considerable uncertainty as to what the next letter might be, and therefore information as to what symbol it actually was would doubtless be very "informative." For the last message, you can be almost certain that the letter N was the one deleted, and again, if you then learn that it was indeed N you will not be much surprised; that is, the symbol N as it appears in the message is not very informative, whereas if it turned out to be L, say, you would be much surprised. Note how uncertainty *prior* to the receipt of the symbol is related to the informativeness of the symbol *after* you have received it: The less certain you are, the more informative the symbol is, but at the same time, the more certain you are, the more informative an unexpected symbol is. Information theory provides a mathematical way of measuring the informativeness of the symbols of a message (and thus of the message as a whole) in terms of the probabilities of those symbols, but it would take too much space to explain this and it is not really necessary for an elementary understanding of information theory ideas.[12]

One important, easily understood idea in information theory is that the amount of information in a symbol is (other things being equal) directly related to the total number of symbols from which one has to choose. If there is only one symbol available, say the letter A, "messages" will be simply strings of A's and the successive symbols can carry no information at all, in the sense defined above. If there are two symbols, say the digits 0 and 1, one will have a 50 per cent chance of guessing each successive symbol in a message composed of a random sequence of such symbols. Each successive symbol will in this case carry one *bit* of information, according to a formula that says the number of bits is the logarithm, to the base 2, of the number of equally-likely alternative symbols. If there are 32 symbols from which one can make random sequences, say the 26 letters of the alphabet plus a space and 5 punctuation marks, this same formula says the number of bits of information carried by each symbol will be 5.

The other important idea in information theory, for our present purposes, is that the amount of information in a symbol is decreased if the symbols are not random but in some degree dependent on (predictable from) each other. We have already seen how the symbol N at the end of the "message" GENERATION carried little if any information, because one could predict it from the previous nine symbols. This idea is important in studying the

[12] See W. R. Garner. *Uncertainty and structure as psychological concepts.* New York: Wiley, 1962.

statistical structure of language, because it allows us to measure the amount of *redundancy* of samples of language text. Redundancy is the property of texts that allows us to predict missing symbols from the context. High-redundancy texts tend to be repetitive and to contain relatively little information per symbol. A text with zero redundancy would be one in which no symbol is predictable from any other, and thus there would be a maximum amount of informativeness per symbol. A list of words selected at random from the dictionary for some purpose would constitute a text with low redundancy.

Psychologists interested in speech production, speech perception, and various problems of verbal learning have found much use for information measurement in their experiments because it provides a precise way of quantifying the amount of material perceived or learned; further, when information is quantified in this way, the relationships discovered are simple and direct. For example, Miller, Heise, and Lichten showed that an individual's ability to identify a word through a considerable amount of noise is inversely related to the logarithm of the number of different words from which he has to choose (see Figure 10). It is not a great jump from this result to the further result that the intelligibility of a word is, other things equal, dependent on the logarithm of its frequency in large samples of verbal material, and it turns out that the amount of "information" (in the technical sense) that one can gain by listening to a single word through noise is approximately constant for words of different frequencies. That is, even though a rare word is identified through noise with difficulty, the average amount of information transmitted by that word, in view of its low frequency of occurrence, is about equal to that transmitted by a common word which can be identified much more easily. These results suggest that the psychological mechanisms whereby stimuli are perceived and learned have built-in limits for handling the informational aspects of stimulation.

This interpretation is also suggested by experiments using samples of language symbols in which the amount of redundancy is artificially controlled, thus controlling the average amount of information in a sample. Samples with various "orders of approximation" to English can be constructed (see Table 3). A zero-order approximation is constructed by stringing out words chosen at random from a dictionary without consideration of their frequency in the language. A first-order approximation is like the zero-order except that the words are chosen in proportion to their frequencies in the language. Second, third, and higher orders of approximation are constructed in a somewhat artificial manner by depending on people's language responses to small strings of symbols. For example, to form a second-order approximation one starts with a word chosen at random, A, and asks someone to use it in a sentence; whatever word, B, follows the given word, A, is used in the string. Then word B is given to another person to be used in a sentence, and whatever word, C, follows B is used as the next word in the approximation. This process is repeated until one has a sufficiently long string of symbols, A, B, C, ... A third-order approximation is constructed by using a set of two words, AB, as stimuli for a sentence to yield a third word C, then using words BC as stimuli to yield D, and so on.

When these artificially contrived language samples are used in experiments,

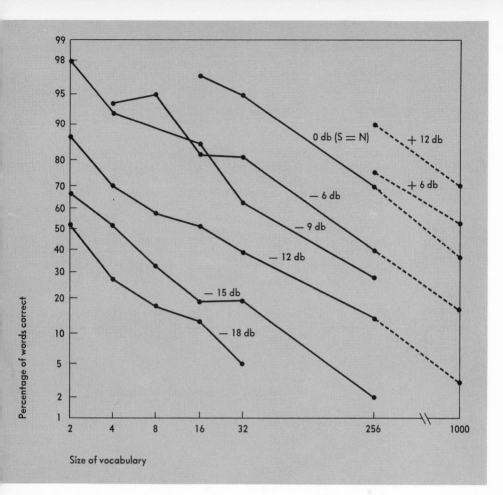

Figure 10. Percentage of words correctly identified as a function of the size of the vocabulary from which they have to be selected, for various signal-to-noise ratios. At 0 db, the signal strength is equal to the noise strength. At +12 db, the signal is 12 decibels (loudness units) above *the noise level, while at −12 db, it is 12 decibels* below *the noise level. (Drawn from data of G. A. Miller, G. A. Heise, and W. Lichten. J. exp. Psychol., 1951, 41, 329–335.)*

it is found that the higher the order of approximation, the easier it is for people to perform various tasks involving the passages—to learn and re-member them, to reconstruct them by guessing, to type them, or to read them aloud. One interpretation of these results is that the response to these complex stimuli depends on the absolute amount of information they contain, and that an individual can readily handle only so much information in a given amount of time. A slightly different interpretation is this: The higher the order of approximation to actual English structure, the more the sample will approximate the particular phonemic, morphemic, and syntactical structures the individual has learned; and it is these structures which correspond to the

TABLE 3

Strings of Words at Various Orders
of Approximation to Normal English Text

Zero order (words chosen at random from a dictionary):

Combat callous irritability migrates depraved temporal prolix alas pillory nautical.

First order (words chosen independently, but with their probability of occurrence proportional to their frequency of occurrence in large samples of normal English text):

Day to is for they have proposed I the it materials of are its go studies the our of the following not over situation if the greater.

Second order (words chosen in such a way that the probability with which each word appears is intended to be proportional to the frequency with which it follows the *one* preceding word in large samples of normal English text):

Goes down here is not large feet are the happy days and so what is dead weight that many were constructed the channel was.

Fourth order (words chosen in such a way that the probability with which each word appears is intended to be proportional to the frequency with which it follows the *three* preceding words in large samples of normal English text):

We are going to see him is not correct to chuckle loudly and depart for home.

As given by G. A. Miller. *Language and communication.* McGraw-Hill, 1951, pp. 84–85.

response habits that function in comprehending and responding to language materials.

We must carefully avoid supposing that frequency counts and information-theory measures throw anything but a faintly reflected light on language structure as it was described in Chapter 2. A language system *as such* has no statistical structure, it being merely a set of regularities of symbolic behavior in a speech community. Frequency counts and information theory are useful in characterizing language samples produced by or experienced by human beings, but they disclose relatively little about the nature of the language systems in which these samples are coded.

THE PERCEPTION AND UNDERSTANDING OF SPEECH

Any thoughtful person who listens to a continuous flow of speech in a language he does not understand will appreciate the astonishing feat performed by the listener in perceiving and interpreting that speech. The listener who knows the language does not hear it as a seemingly random concatenation of sounds. Instead, from the sound waves, he is able to select and respond to particular units of various sizes.

There has been a great deal of investigation, for obvious practical reasons, concerning what can be done to a speech wave and still leave the speech message it bears reasonably intelligible to a person who can understand the original message. For example, how much noise and interference can safely be added to the speech wave? In what way can the speech wave be distorted? The detailed results of these studies cannot be presented here, but one important conclusion from them can: namely, that the speech wave is highly redundant. Not every part of the speech wave is a completely new, independent bit of information; instead, some parts are repetitions of signals presented previously, or at least they are predictable from the signals by anybody who has learned to interpret those messages. Thus, if noise or distortion is introduced, the chances are that enough information will come through to enable the hearer to infer the whole message. In fact, the intelligibility of speech is amazingly resistant to distortions of a speech wave.

A speech wave would have a certain amount of redundancy even if the message contained nothing more than nonsense syllables. But it will contain much more redundancy if normal speech samples are used. It has been estimated that the redundancy of normal speech samples is probably better than 50 per cent.

There are many sources of redundancy. Among them are these: phonemes vary in frequency (therefore, a missing phoneme is more likely to be a common one than a rare one); phonemes cannot be strung out randomly (for example, a string of consonant phonemes can be only so long before it has to be followed by a vowel); the inventory of morphemes in our language does not include all the possible combinations of phonemes; morphemes themselves vary in frequency; morphemes cannot be strung out randomly—they have to be put in grammatical sentences; and finally, there are practical limitations on the things we are likely to say—a sentence like "The sieve larch was then dissimilar in neither miracle" is highly unlikely though grammatical.

The more redundancy in a message, the greater the chance that it will be understood despite noise, electronic distortion of the signal, or low speech volume or poor intelligibility of the speaker. But redundancy is helpful only to the extent that the hearer is able to take advantage of it. If the listener doesn't know the structure of the language, or has no feeling for what is likely to be said, redundancy is not very helpful. The speech in an airport control tower is statistically highly redundant, but in noise it is practically unintelligible to the uninitiated.

Even without noise, speech signals have to be sufficiently discriminable to allow the hearer to recognize the units of the message. For normal speakers and hearers, phonemes are rarely confused, even though they may be very close in sheer acoustic terms. It will not do to appeal solely to redundancy or context to explain this lack of confusion; the phonemes themselves are distinguishable even in minimal pairs. In fact, evidence suggests that for the speakers of a given language, phonemes have *acquired distinctiveness;* that is, the speakers have learned to discriminate classes of sounds, even though they may be indiscriminable to speakers of other languages.[13] Further, it appears that for certain kinds of phonemic distinctions, hearers' sensitivity is heightened in those regions along acoustic dimensions that are most critical in making those distinctions. For example, subjects clearly discriminate the

[13] A. M. Liberman, K. S. Harris, H. S. Hoffman, and B. C. Griffith. *J. exp. Psychol.,* 1957, 54, 358–368.

small changes along the dimensions that produce the differences among /b, d, g/, but fail to discriminate changes of equal magnitude, elsewhere on those dimensions, that do not happen to produce a phonemic difference.

There is a possible psychological significance in the fact that the number of segmental phonemes in languages varies from about 12 to 65; with 33 phonemes, English stands at about the median. A language cannot have too few phonemes, because with a very small number, the morphemes of the language would have to be longer, on the average, to be distinctive, and they might not be readily remembered; on the other hand, a language cannot have too many phonemes, because the phonemes themselves might be less easily discriminable.

The rate of normal uninterrupted English speech is about 165 words per minute; because average word length may vary, perhaps *syllables* per minute would be a better measure; that figure is about 265 syllables per minute. If the hearer of such speech knows the language adequately—that is, if he knows the grammar and the lexicon used—he would probably report that he can "understand" speech at this rate. By use of a special device for speeding up tape-recorded speech without changing its pitch (the latter would happen if one simply increased the speed of the tape) it has been found that speech is still intelligible when presented at up to 2.5 times normal rates. (At 450 words per minute, this rate is still below that at which printed words can be read and understood.) Actually, comprehensibility is a very difficult thing to measure objectively; one has to depend largely on the listener's subjective report as to whether he can "follow" speech presented at an accelerated rate. The comprehensibility of speeded speech would also depend both on the characteristics of the speech itself—the complexity of its grammar, the difficulty of the vocabulary used, and the abstractness or technicality of the content— and on the competence of the listener. Nevertheless, it seems clear that in many cases it would be possible through the use of speeded speech to transmit information much more efficiently than usual.

How does a listener understand speech, whatever its rate may be? We have likened a sentence to a "program" for a computing machine by calling it a computer program for a thinking machine, that is, the human central nervous system. Unlike a true computer program, where the smallest error may lead to a complete stoppage, sentences have enough redundancy so that even if they contain "errors" like "slips of the tongue," they will normally still be understood.

Whereas the speaker formulates his utterances *first* by selecting major sentence-types and transformations and *then* by filling them in with appropriate forms, the listener must apply these procedures in reverse order, as it were. That is, all that is available to him is the sequence of forms; from this he must "construe" the sentence in some particular grammatical pattern. Occasionally, the heard sentence will be constructionally ambiguous and permit two or more interpretations, and he may guess wrong even in the presence of adequate context. For example, *the exploitation of the workers* might be construed as a transformation of (*they*) *exploit workers* when it was intended as a transformation of *workers exploit*. But the very fact that the listener chooses *an* interpretation demonstrates the potency of grammatical structure. Generally, the over-all pattern of a sentence in English can be detected rather early in the sentence. The form-classes of the first few words in a sentence usually indicate, for example, whether it is to be an existence-assertion or a predication, and whether it is in a null, a question, an imperative, or some other kind of transformation.

We may regard each decoded grammatical construction as a discriminative stimulus for some response in the listener. We must assume that these responses are covert, not immediately observable by any normal means. For example, a null transformation is a discriminative stimulus for an orienting response to note the information contained in the utterance; a question transformation is a discriminative stimulus to search for the information requested by the question-signal (an auxiliary verb, in the case of a yes-no question, or a *"wh*-word" in the case of a multiple-response question), and so forth.

O. Hobart Mowrer has proposed that a sentence in the predicate form (like *Tom is a thief*) is an arrangement for conditioning the meaning response produced by the predicate *is a thief* to the meaning response to the subject *Tom.* That is to say, the meaning reaction to *is a thief* now gets connected to the meaning reaction produced by *Tom,* and the hearer's subsequent behavior in the presence of Tom may bear this out. Mowrer's proposal is interesting and probably on the right track; it is very limited, however, for a *particular* utterance can hardly be a "conditioning arrangement" unless one ignores evidence that conditioning rarely occurs in one trial; more importantly, it fails to do justice to the complexities of sentence construction. How, for example, shall we deal with a sentence like *Tom is not a thief*? Could the word *not* cancel the conditioning arrangement so facilely?

According to the evidence as we see it, a sentence is a series of discriminative stimuli, learned by the speaker of a language, which in effect "program" the mediating responses of the hearer in such a way that certain constructions are put on the sentence and corresponding mediating responses are evoked in the hearer. If A hears B say, "Tom is a thief," this sentence is a series of discriminative stimuli for mediating responses that represent:

1. a predication
2. a declaration (it being in the null transformation) on the part of B; that is, A learns that B entertains a belief about Tom
3. *Tom* (the context supplies information as to which Tom is meant)
4. *is:* present tense, current predicative
5. *a thief* (one of a class of thieves)

or some such list.

In countries with formal systems of education, the age at which children learn to read is somewhere between five and seven, fixed more by tradition than by any rational considerations of the best age to start to read. A few children manage to learn to read before they go to school—often with minimal help from others; a fairly substantial number of other children are delayed in their progress; and, of course, there are those who do not have the opportunity to learn to read until they are adults, if then. But psychological considerations, and evidence from a number of educational experiments, suggest that children *can* be taught to read as soon as they have gained mastery of essential features of the spoken language, its phonology, its most common grammatical constructions, and a basic vocabulary. (Whether such early reading is desirable from a developmental point of view cannot be debated here.)

What, really, do we mean by "reading"? A written text is a representation of a possible spoken utterance. Except for special phonetic transcriptions devised by linguists, writing systems give an imperfect representation of the actual sounds produced in a spoken utterance. To be sure, some writing systems, like those of Spanish or Finnish, convey fairly accurately the *segmental* phonemes, but no writing system represents suprasegmental phonemes at all adequately. Only an individual who has a considerable mastery of the spoken language is able to infer how a written text might reasonably be spoken, from the limited cues supplied by the text and its punctuation. (This is another case of the use of context to supply missing data in a message.) We can define reading, ultimately, as the activity of reconstructing (overtly or covertly) a reasonable spoken message from a printed text, and making meaning responses to the reconstructed message that would parallel those that would be made to the spoken message. (Recall our discussion of how it is that we comprehend a spoken message.)

The learning of reading, defined in this way, is obviously something that may take a considerable amount of time. We take it for granted that normally a learner has already attained some control of the spoken language before he tries to learn to read, although there are many situations throughout the world where the learning of reading is attended with particular difficulty because the child is asked to read a language not his own before he has sufficiently mastered the spoken form of that language.

One major goal in learning to read is to learn to respond to written texts in accordance with the writing *system*, that is, in accordance with any regular or partially regular correspondences between spoken sounds and written symbols that may exist in this system. The standard orthographies or conventional writing systems associated with various languages (some languages have two or three such systems) vary in the simplicity and regularity of these correspondences; most of them use an alphabetic principle whereby phonemes are directly represented in written symbols. In the case of some languages, like Finnish, Spanish, and Turkish, these correspondences are simple and highly regular; since they can be learned quite readily, this aspect of the task of learning to read can be made relatively easy. At the opposite extreme is the orthography of Japanese, where three parallel systems of orthography, only two of which are even partially phonemic, must be learned.

The standard orthography of the English language presents a peculiar problem. It is incorrect to say that English is "unphonetic." This adjective cannot be applied to a language, in any case, because languages necessarily have phonetic aspects; nor can it properly be applied to a writing system, because writing systems are dependent more on the phonemic than the phonetic properties of the languages they represent. The grapheme-phoneme correspondences of English orthography are somewhat irregular, although not as irregular as one might think. It is possible to formulate a set of rules for "translating" a printed text into segmental phonemes so that more than 95 per cent of the phonemes would be correct. The rules would be fairly complicated; one of them might be, for example, that the letter C followed by E or I is to be translated by the phoneme /s/, unless E or I is followed by a further vowel letter, in which case it will correspond to /š/.

A great deal of argument and a limited amount of study and experimentation have been devoted to the question of how the reading of English can best be taught in view of the facts about its orthography. It is recognized that a child *can* be taught to respond correctly to whole words, with no reference to the sound correspondences of their letters; the argument is over how early in reading instruction the child can be taught to take advantage of such correspondences. One widespread opinion (actually a misinterpretation of certain research studies) is that a child cannot be so taught until he has a mental age of about seven, but this is demonstrably false, for many children do learn to read in terms of grapheme-phoneme correspondences well before they attain this mental age.

Apparently, the way in which these grapheme-phoneme correspondences is introduced is important. The learner needs to be presented with systematic sets of instances from which he can readily learn the discriminative function of those letters or combinations of letters which are fairly sure guides to pronunciation. For example, at some point the child needs to see that there is a regularity in such pairs as *at-ate, fat-fate, hat-hate, mat-mate,* not by learning rules or verbalizing them, but by achieving consistent discriminative responses. At the same time he needs to learn that he must often adopt a somewhat experimental trial-and-error approach to the letter combinations in words like *come, dome, home, some.* He must also be taught to take account of context in such experimentation, or educated guessing.

Concern with grapheme-phoneme correspondences, or "phonics" as it is often called, should not distract us from the necessity for the reader to attain a rapid visual perception of printed words *as wholes*. It is probably wise to give some training and practice in this in the earliest stages of reading, by means of a "sight vocabulary." (The sight vocabulary, however, can be chosen so as to take optimum advantage of the regularities that exist in English orthography while catering to the learner's need to know common "irregular" words like *the, to, what*.) Experiments in visual pattern perception suggest that recognition of words as visual patterns can be accelerated by (1) drawing attention to the shapes of the parts of these patterns, that is, the letters, (2) giving practice in writing or tracing these parts, and (3) building up the frequency of exposure to these patterns. By means of the tachistoscope (a rapid-exposure device), it can be shown that mature readers recognize common words in not much more time than they need to recognize single letters, around one-tenth of a second. Other things being equal, recognition time appears to be inversely related to the frequency with which a word has been seen by a reader in his past reading (see Figure 11). These results suggest that each word in a basic reading vocabulary should be presented many times over. At the same time, vocabulary control need not go so far as to exclude words that the beginning reader can interpret on the basis of the phonic habits he has built up.

Efficient reading entails well-coordinated eye movements of the saccadic variety (the ones by which the eyes jump from one fixation to another). At

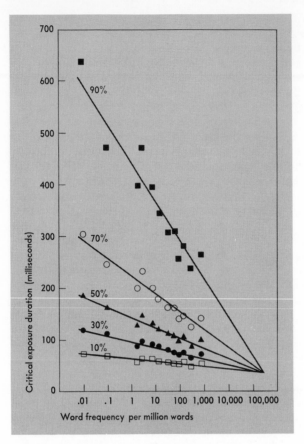

Figure 11. The relationship between word frequency and speed of tachistoscopic perception. Each set of points shows the average amount of exposure time (milliseconds) required by 20 subjects to recognize words of the indicated frequencies with a given percentage of accuracy. (Adapted from data of D. Howes. In J. Money (ed.). Reading disability. *Baltimore: Johns Hopkins Press, 1962.)*

one time it was thought that reading could be improved by training these eye movements themselves, but it now appears that poor eye movements are an effect, not a cause. Mechanical devices for pacing reading performance are valuable mainly for arousing effort and attention on the part of the learner; they are of little use if the learner has not acquired the basic perceptual responses which are prerequisite to rapid reading.

In the mature reader, reading speeds are a function of the reader's training, his purpose in reading (light skimming and concentrated study are at opposite poles of a continuum), and the difficulty of the material. There are various ways to measure the difficulty, or "readability," of prose. One is to use one of the several formulas that have been developed, dependent usually on crude measures of the grammatical complexity and vocabulary level of the material. Another is the "cloze" procedure developed by Wilson Taylor, whereby the readability of a passage is evaluated by deleting, say, every tenth word in a text and seeing how successful, on the average, the members of a panel of readers are in guessing the missing words from the context. As compared with formulas, the latter procedure seems more successful, for example, in detecting that the prose of Gertrude Stein is fairly difficult despite her use of common words and sentences of moderate length.

Because of the many factors in reading speed, definite standards have little meaning unless one specifies the purpose of reading, the difficulty of the material to be read, and the method of measuring comprehension. There is probably a certain limit to the rate at which verbal information in any form can be taken in by a human being. If we take as a standard the degree of comprehension that can be attained when material is presented orally at a normal rate (say 165 words, or 265 syllables, per minute), the rate at which an individual can *read* material of the same difficulty with the same degree of comprehension will probably not be over three or four times the speech rate (that is, not over 500–700 words per minute). (Strangely, there is no research evidence that has given a reliable and sensible answer to this problem; the few research reports available confuse comprehension with memory for details.) When reading rates much higher than this are reported, they are probably attained with a lower standard of comprehension or with greater than normal use of redundancy and context. The claim that reading speed and comprehension are positively correlated is true only up to a point, and only within groups of people whose *average* reading ability is well below reasonable standards. In the case of a poor reader, reading speed can hardly be improved without improving comprehension as well. Comprehension, in turn, is improved by teaching the reader not only to recognize words faster, but also to respond more swiftly to the grammatical signals in a piece of prose and to attain a wider and richer vocabulary.

Individual Differences
in Language Behavior

The members of a speech community obviously differ greatly in their ability to use and understand language. Our most precise information about these differences comes from the study of performances in the more or less controlled situations we call *tests*. The so-called *intelligence* tests probably enjoy the widest general use, and a major class of these are *verbal* intelligence tests, which measure an individual's understanding of words and his ability to manipulate and apply abstract verbal concepts. There are, in addition, many other kinds of tests involving language habits: free association tests, sentence completion tests, articulation

66

5

tests, reading readiness tests, foreign language aptitude tests, and so forth.

The old concept that "intelligence" is a general trait or characteristic of the individual has given way to the notion that the classification of human abilities into various "traits" is a somewhat arbitrary operation, justifiable only when it can be demonstrated that the behaviors classified under a given trait tend to occur together more often than would be expected by chance. Even after we have demonstrated that they do, we still have the problem of explaining this result. The behaviors may have been learned together, for some fortuitous reason, or there may be some common explanation for their co-occurrence, such as a single genetic trait that makes them both possible.

In studying differences in language ability, therefore, we should start with the widest possible sampling of language performances and see whether there are any systematic ways in which the members of a speech community vary with respect to these performances. We must then see what explanations for these systematic differences we can find.

Information about the basic dimensions on which people vary has been provided largely by the statistical technique known as factor analysis. This is a procedure for studying the intercorrelations of measures that are applied to representative samples of people or things to identify the basic ways in which these people or things differ. Each such way can be called a dimension or *factor*. Combing the results of a number of studies, we find the following kinds of more or less independent dimensions of ability in the domain of language behavior.

1. *Verbal knowledge.* One of the most pervasive ways in which people differ is in their knowledge of the vocabulary and structure of the English language. This dimension of ability is measured in greater or lesser degree by the following types of tests: vocabulary tests (in fact any test in which attainment depends to a considerable extent on knowledge of the meanings of words, particularly the rarer and more abstract words); tests of knowledge of "correct" (that is, socially approved) English grammar and usage; spelling tests (to the extent that they involve more difficult vocabulary); and certain tests of sentence completion that are scored for the extent to which people's responses agree with those of the majority. Verbal knowledge is highly correlated with the extent, variety, and richness of an individual's concepts, at least to the extent that these concepts are symbolized by words.

2. *Abstract reasoning abilities.* Although the factor analysis of reasoning abilities has given results that are somewhat ambiguous and variously interpreted, it seems clear that people differ markedly in their ability to perform reasoning tasks, whether concrete or abstract. Some results suggest that inductive reasoning ability is somewhat independent of deductive ability, and that both in turn are independent of serial reasoning ability—the ability to think through a chain of inferential reasoning steps.

3. *Ideational fluency.* This factor represents an individual's facility in

calling up as many ideas as possible about a given topic or theme; the number of different ideas, rather than their quality, is at issue. A typical test of this ability is the one in which subjects are asked to write down as fast as possible the words for as many "round things" as they can think of in a brief time.

4. *Word fluency.* This ability is something like ideational fluency, but concerns the ability to think of words with certain formal characteristics— such as those beginning with certain letters when spelled. It seems to depend partly on the individual's knowledge of phoneme-grapheme correspondences, and also possibly on what we may call "phonemic coding ability," that is, the ability to encode what is heard into a form that can be put in a memory storage and used at a later time. Certain tests of word fluency and of phonemic coding ability have been very successful in predicting facility in learning a foreign language.

5. *Fluency of expression.* This factor represents the individual's facility in formulating ideas—that is, given an idea, his facility in putting it in grammatically acceptable words and constructions. It can be tested in various ways; one is to ask the individual to think up a large number of expressions for praising the virtues of a political candidate.

6. *Grammatical sensitivity.* This is the ability to recognize the functions of form-classes and constructions and to perform tasks requiring the ability to perceive these functions. It is an important factor in aptitude for learning a foreign language.

7. *Naming facility.* This factor represents the ability to respond rapidly with the names of things, shapes, colors, and so on, when a series of such items is presented in rapid succession.

8. *Oral speech ability.* This represents ability to speak effectively and coherently in a more or less formal speaking situation.

9. *Articulation ability.* This represents individual differences in the speed with which speech sounds or utterances are, or can be, articulated.

This list of language abilities is by no means exhaustive, and remains to be clarified by further research.

Many of these factors have great practical significance in education and personnel selection. Because verbal knowledge and reasoning abilities are so advantageous in scholastic work, typical verbal intelligence tests, such as the Scholastic Aptitude Test of the College Entrance Examination Board, tend to stress the measurement of these abilities, along with quantitative reasoning abilities. Several of the factors are of unique importance in the learning of foreign languages, as indicated above, and are measured by the Modern Language Aptitude Test. But some of the other kinds of ability we have listed have not as yet shown any important relation to any kind of practical work. Contrary to expectation, for example, the fluency of expression factor seems to be unrelated to skill in English composition.

What about the causation or etiology of these individual differences in learning ability? To the extent that some of these abilities are included in what we usually call "intelligence," this question about causation might require us to discuss what it is that spreads human beings out on the scale from genius to idiocy, but there are more appropriate places than this for such a discussion. Certainly both genetic and environmental influences are at work.

There has been relatively little research on the possible hereditary etiology of those aspects of language ability that are largely independent of intelligence. We have some evidence of a genetic basis for the special difficulties that a certain small percentage of children, particularly males, have with beginning reading and spelling, and later, with learning of foreign languages, even though the children may be otherwise quite intelligent. This syndrome is called *specific language disability* and is characterized by difficulty in encoding and storing auditory (phonetic) information and tying it with visual symbols. It may have a close relation to the word fluency factor mentioned earlier.

For the most part, we can probably attribute individual differences in verbal abilities to environmental influences—differential opportunities to learn language behavior, and differential conditions of motivational arousal and reinforcement. For example, individual differences in the verbal knowledge factor are clearly related to socio-economic status, amount of schooling, parents' occupations, and other variables that indirectly measure opportunity and motivation to learn language. This seems plausible since the full development of native language skills, even though the groundwork is laid in early childhood, requires the whole period of childhood and adolescence. In fact, the acquisition of vocabulary is a process that goes on to some degree even in old age. Because vocabulary knowledge is little disturbed even in senility, the relative degree to which certain other abilities are lost is claimed to be an indication of intellectual deterioration.

LANGUAGE IN MENTAL RETARDATION

In the early years of life, some children are slow in learning to talk. Such retardation can mean any one of a number of things. Sometimes the retardation is associated with a pattern of growth in which motor development runs ahead of mental development. Sometimes it is psychogenic—that is, the result of emotional problems or unfortunate learning sequences. But it may also mean that the child is mentally retarded due to some organic or constitutional defect in the nervous system. Certainly delayed or arrested language development is one of the most universal characteristics of mental retardation when properly diagnosed. Idiots, with IQ's below 20, rarely attain any language use beyond a small number of isolated words and the comprehension of simple commands. In other grades of retardation, language development is delayed in proportion to the extent of mental deficiency. Even the babbling stage is delayed. One study reported that in children with an IQ of 51 to 70, babbling occurred, on the average, at 20.8 months, word use at 34.5 months, and sentence use at 89.4 months. The corresponding figures for a normal child would be, approximately, 4 months, 12 months, and 20 months. Along with these late starts one finds, of course, very low ceilings of development; a child with an IQ of 50 will on the average rise only to a mental age of 7 or 8; language usage of such a child is restricted to relatively simple sentences and a vocabulary of a few hundred words. There is, however, a class of "educable mentally retarded" children who can be taught to read and write up to somewhere between grades three and seven. IQ's for such

Individual
Differences
in Language
Behavior

children range from 50 to 75. But all these children have considerable trouble with language, with both its motor and its conceptual aspects. Speech defects are especially common, and difficult to remedy.

The study of the slow-motion language development of mental defectives might throw much light on how grammar develops and how various grammatical phenomena rank themselves in conceptual difficulty.

Aphasia (etymologically, "lack of speech") is a term that is ordinarily applied to a condition in which a person who has already acquired language competence suddenly and dramatically loses some or all of this competence because of brain damage. The appropriateness of this term in the case of what is sometimes called "childhood aphasia" is somewhat questionable, although there is indeed a condition in children, distinguishable from mental retardation, where delay in language development is associated with some specific kind of brain injury or maldevelopment resulting from prenatal condition or birth trauma. Here, we shall focus attention on aphasia in adults.

The language disturbances found in aphasia are exceedingly diverse, and of differing degrees of severity. Some patients lose all capability of speaking and understanding, but most have residual capacity in certain performances. Early classifications of aphasia were not based on a sufficient number of cases or on sufficiently comprehensive clinical examinations. At present, it is widely accepted that there are no distinct "types" of aphasia, although it is recognized that cases differ not only in severity but also in kinds of loss. In some cases the loss seems to lie predominantly in speech "reception" (recognition and understanding), whereas in others, defect is manifested chiefly in a reduced ability to express thoughts. Among the latter, some are chiefly handicapped by an inability to find particular words for concepts (anomia), and others by incapacity to form coherent sentences (syntactical aphasia).

Aphasic disorders may also be accompanied by deficits in visual and spatial perception—for example, inability to recognize common objects and symbols, or to recognize the equivalence of stimuli. Poor control of the speech musculature, even inability to swallow, may occur in some cases. But a central characteristic of all aphasias is loss of ability to conceptualize and to manipulate concepts by language symbols, or as Kurt Goldstein puts it, a loss of ability to use abstractions and to generalize. The nature of this loss can be better understood when it is recognized that the aphasic loses not only the ability to express himself by language—he also loses the ability to express himself by gestures or other symbolic movements, or to understand such gestures when others try to use them in communicating with him.

Some psychologists have been tempted to use these diverse patterns of aphasia to throw light on the possible neural mechanisms and organization underlying language behavior. Charles Osgood has postulated a model of language behavior as a multistage process that involves three levels: a *projection* level at which stimuli are "projected" in appropriate areas of the brain; an *integrative* level in which these stimuli are recognized and integrated with other stimuli in appropriate grammatical constructions; and a *representational*

Individual
Differences
in Language
Behavior

level at which the significances of language signs are recognized and manipulated. The model also assumes three processes in the handling of information: decoding, association, and encoding, each of which can operate at each of the three levels of organization just mentioned. Aphasic symptoms, according to Osgood, represent losses of function at one or more of these levels and in one or more of these processes, and he has had fair success in making the symptoms of individual cases of aphasia fit this model. Some of the results from the work of neurologists and brain surgeons support Osgood's general point of view, but other investigators still incline to the belief that the phenomena of aphasia are too complex to be dealt with in this way. For example, one school of thought, represented by Davis Howes, holds that most of the phenomena of aphasia can be explained as due to a general loss of the strength of verbal habits. A closely related opinion is that of Hildred Schuell and James Jenkins, who hold that aphasia is a unitary phenomenon characterized by general loss of language competence on both the receptive and the productive side; accompaniments of aphasia such as disturbances in visual perception and poor control of speech musculature are not essentially aphasia, for they can occur without aphasia.

Despite very active research on the subject, our notions of the nature of aphasia are still quite indefinite. Fortunately, lack of agreement on the theory of aphasia has not impeded the development of therapeutic procedures. Therapy usually requires considerable time, but can be successful in many cases. Apparently relearning often involves the development of new neural pathways for language functions.

LANGUAGE IN ABNORMAL MENTAL STATES

In practically every form of neurosis or psychosis, there is some alteration or disturbance of speech and language behavior. From the mildest type of neurosis, in which the patient may express his anxieties by a slightly abnormal repetitiousness of speech, or by noticeable hesitations or speech blocks, to severe schizophrenias in which speech is fantastically garbled in what is often called "word salad," we have evidence that these abnormal mental states can influence both the form and the content of speech. On the other hand, all these behaviors represent extreme forms of phenomena that occur in normal individuals—slips of the tongue, overrepetition of certain words and phrases, and even garbled speech. They apparently represent lapses in attention and in the central control of speech processes, as well as the operation of motivational dynamics. Freud presented a classic account of how slips of the tongue may often be interpreted as evidences for repressed motives. The "word salad" speech of the schizophrenic can be regarded as the result of three tendencies: (1) the disorganization of syntactical behavior, that is, an extreme form of the kind of disorganization that occurs when we make false starts and change the grammatical construction of a sentence; (2) paranomia, the tendency to replace the ordinary names for things with substitute names— neologisms and other highly personal symbols; and (3) a heightened lability of verbal association. The first tendency is understandable enough when thought itself is disorganized; the second may be the result of fearsome or aversive associations evoked by the ordinary names of things (analogous to taboo words) or an unconscious motivation to construct a personal idiosyncratic language system which sets the patient apart from others. The third tendency accentuates the kind of free-wheeling association that can be produced by alcohol and certain drugs, or even in certain states of religious ecstasy, when the normal inhibitions against absurd or trivial intraverbal connections are released. Despite such deviations in language form and content, there is little evidence that patients ever lose the underlying phonology and grammar of their language. Speech disturbances can be looked upon as a special kind of transformation of language habits.

STUTTERING

Stuttering (also called stammering) is a disorder of speech that makes its appearance in some small proportion of children (estimates range from 1 to 5 per cent), usually about the age of two to four years. It has been defined as "a disturbance of rhythm and fluency of speech by an intermittent blocking, a convulsive repetition, or prolongation of sounds, syllables, words, phrases, or posture of speech organs." Incidence is somewhat higher in boys than in girls.

In view of all the research that has been devoted to the matter, it is surprising that there is no generally accepted, single explanation for stuttering. It is evidently a disorder of the motor control of speech. Theories of stuttering focus either on heredity or environment. Environmental theories stress either organic (neurological or chemical) factors or functional (psychogenic) etiology. Those who prefer functionalist theories assert that stuttering arises when circumstances make a young child anxious about his speech—that is, fearful that he will not be able to speak properly. It is claimed that the very existence of the concept of stuttering channels the behavior of parents and teachers into unwittingly fostering the development of stuttering out of the normal speech errors that nearly every child makes. This theory has been neither confirmed nor disproved by the research results available thus far; it seems prudent to recommend, however, that in raising children parents should avoid creating anxiety concerning minor speech errors. But it is also possible that stuttering is an accompaniment of anxieties and conflicts that are deeper than a mere concern with speech behavior. In many cases, successful cures of stuttering in adolescents and adults have been effected by protracted psychotherapy in which the patient is enabled to rid himself of intense conflicts, often concerned with matters of self-identity, sex-typing, and psychological maturity.

Stuttering can also be analyzed and treated simply as a motor response, associated with the effort of uttering a syllable. There has been some success, for example, in treating it as an operant response and putting it under the control of rewarding or aversive stimulation.[1] The stimulation is provided by an unpleasant sound presented by earphones; a stutter can be *rewarded* by turning off this sound momentarily as soon as the stutter appears, or it can be

[1] B. Flanagan, I. Goldiamond, and N. Azrin. *J. exper. anal. Behav.*, 1958, 1, 173–177.

punished by turning on this sound momentarily. As might be expected, reward increases the incidence of stuttering beyond the individual's normal rate, and punishment decreases it. However, the effects are restricted to the experimental situation, and are not startling. A much more dramatic effect has been obtained by C. Cherry and B. M. Sayers in England.[2] They claim that stuttering can often be totally inhibited, in an experimental situation, by what they call a "shadowing technique" in which the stutterer is asked to say aloud, as close to simultaneously as possible, what he hears another person say or read aloud. A variant of the procedure is to have the stutterer read a passage aloud with another person; the stammering is reduced or absent even if the other person starts reading something else, or saying gibberish. Cherry and Sayers interpret these results as indicating that stammering can be reduced by distracting the stutterer's attention from his own voice. They also have shown that stammering can usually be totally inhibited by using a white noise (a noise containing all frequencies of the audible range) to mask out the normal feedback from the voice to the ear provided by bone-conduction. These findings give promise of helping us work out a better theory of the motor aspects of speech production, and this may eventually point the way towards more reliable therapy for stuttering than is now available.

LANGUAGE IN DEAF CHILDREN

The development of language in children who are congenitally deaf or suffer a marked hearing loss *before* they acquire speech raises two particularly interesting theoretical questions: (1) Since these children may have normal or even superior intellectual functioning, what kind of intellectual functioning and symbolic behavior do they have prior to the acquisition of true language responses? And (2) since language responses have to be acquired without the normal dependence on sound, can the language fluency of normal speech ever be attained without this dependence, and if so, by what means? Of secondary but by no means insignificant interest are the sign or gesture languages that are often learned and used among the deaf as an apparently normal means of communication (in fact almost as "mother tongues") and the teaching of lip-reading.

Deaf children who have not acquired language, not even a sign language, can perform nearly all of the perceptual and cognitive tasks that hearing children of roughly comparable ages can perform, as long as these tasks do not involve language in any way. Any retardation that deaf children may show (typically, development is delayed by about one year) is likely to be due to the fact that their experiences of the world are inevitably limited in certain ways; it is not necessarily due to the absence of language. Research by Hans Furth in America and by Pierre Oléron in France has rather well established that deaf children without language can acquire concepts, compare magnitudes, remember sequences and associations, and solve simple problems involving forms, colors, and the like. These performances are generally well above the level of cognitive functioning that can be secured from primates.

[2] C. Cherry and B. M. Sayers. *J. psychosom. Res.,* 1956, 1, 233–246.

These findings suggest strongly that there *can* be a kind of "thought" without language, and this possibility will have to be kept in mind during the ensuing discussion of the relationship of language and thought.

The task of teaching a deaf child to speak has been called one of the most difficult teaching tasks there is; in fact, from ancient times up to about the eighteenth century it was believed impossible, and deaf children were treated essentially like idiots. The completely deaf person has no proper way of monitoring his own performance; kinesthetic-tactual feedback is a far cry from the auditory feedback upon which the hearing person depends. Furthermore, this kinesthetic-tactual feedback bears virtually no relation to the visual stimulation the deaf person has to use to interpret what is spoken to him by others. Lipreading, or "speech reading" as it has come to be called (because it involves more than just the lips), is at best a difficult and somewhat unreliable form of communication, since many phonemic contrasts of auditory language disappear and a great many words are in effect homonyms. For example, the phonemes /m, b, p/ are visually identical, and therefore the speech reader must rely heavily on context and probabilities to distinguish such words as *mill, bill, pill*. It is nevertheless possible to teach a deaf person to speak with fair intelligibility, and to understand the spoken language of others. The learning process is exceedingly slow and arduous. The evidence strongly suggests that it is not merely a truism that the critical difficulty for the deaf in learning language is their inability to hear large amounts of language *spoken*. No amount of reading of written language seems to be able to fill this gap; the grammatical patterns of printed words cannot impress themselves on the mind as in spoken language. This conclusion adds force to the conviction that writing cannot serve as an independent system of communication. It is interesting to note, however, that the manual sign system of the deaf does function as a normal system of communication; it has a grammatical and semantic structure of its own. That it is often learned by deaf children considerably later than the normal period of first language learning seems to indicate, contrary to the opinion which has sometimes been expressed, that the normal age of learning language (say, from age one to age four) is not a maturational "critical period" in the sense that language not learned at that time will never be learned.

Cognition and Thinking

In this chapter we are going to talk about the psychological analysis of a series of concepts that we refer to every day with such words as *knowing, thinking,* and *believing.* Ordinary language does not yield any precise conceptions of the denotations of these words. Take a word like *think*: Consider the variety of meanings denoted in the following contexts.

I'm just thinking. . . . What do you think about him? . . . I wish I had thought of that possibility. . . . I think he'll come soon. . . . I couldn't think of his name. . . . He was thinking of his childhood. . . . I think that person is insane. . . . Think this through carefully. . . .

75

6

The root meaning here seems to be "some kind of covert (unobservable) behavior in response to stimuli that may be absent, not immediately present to the senses." But in some of the above sentences the word has overtones of *belief,* or *remembrance,* or *expectation,* or *mental discovery.* Often, too, it implies some kind of self-generated, more or less prolonged covert activity oriented towards a desired outcome such as a plan of action, a piece of writing, or the solution of a problem. The layman is usually concerned with all these kinds of thinking: He wants to think "correctly" or more "efficiently," to solve problems more swiftly, or to make ingenious mental discoveries when he searches for them. To ask the psychologist for prescriptions to improve thinking, however, is like asking an engineer for suggestions for improving the process of locomotion. Just as the engineer could only give help if he is asked about specific kinds of locomotion and the specific conditions that might obtain, so the psychologist cannot say much about a general concept like thinking unless specific kinds of thinking are at issue.

This is also the problem when the question of the relation between language and thought is raised. Obviously, many kinds of "thinking" are non-linguistic. Some musicians report being able to "listen" to the music they are composing, before writing it down on paper or even playing it on an instrument; this sort of activity would qualify as a nonlinguistic kind of thinking, and there are parallels in other spheres of activity—for instance, thinking through a planned aerial maneuver, a swimming stroke, or a dance step. In fact, we may lay it down as a proposition that any kind of behavior that can be observed overtly may also be represented in covert form. Overt speech can therefore be represented in what is sometimes called "inner speech."

Even the process of recognition is a form of covert, unobservable behavior, as was pointed out in Chapter 3 (p. 35). We can, of course, often obtain overt, verbal reports of what is recognized, but that recognition is inherently a covert process seems to be a reasonable conclusion from the fact that under certain conditions we can obtain a verbal report concerning the recognition of a stimulus which is not objectively present. For example, hungry people will sometimes report seeing faint pictures of foods when they are actually shown nothing but a blank screen, and subjects can also be induced to report recognition of words in a tachistoscopic experiment even when the exposure contains no words at all.[1]

If, therefore, recognition of external stimuli is a covert process, which may or may not be overtly reported (and an overt report may or may not be verbal—it may consist simply of pressing a key), it is an easy step to the notion that there may also be recognition and processing of *internal* stimuli. One of the most challenging tasks for the experimental psychologist is to obtain objective evidence for such internal responses—at least, to build a sufficiently water-tight case for the inferred existence of such responses, if they exist.

Early behaviorists like Watson actually assumed the existence of such

[1] I. Goldiamond and W. F. Hawkins. *J. exp. Psychol.,* 1958, 56, 457–463. These investigators showed, incidentally, that even when the exposures were blank the subjects tended to report words (nonsense syllables) in proportion to the frequency with which they had experienced them in prior learning trials.

responses, but assumed them to be the reduced action of the speech musculature. This theory provoked a series of experiments to find out whether thought
activity could go on without any kind of response detectable by electronic
monitoring of the musculature. The net result of this series of investigations,
which were plagued by almost insuperable methodological difficulties, was
to support the propositions that mental activity occurs in the central nervous
system and that it need not be accompanied by activity in the motor system.
It was demonstrated that perceptual and thinking activities could occur and
be remembered even when the motor system of an individual is completely
immobilized by a drug of the curare family. When activity *is* detected in the
motor system, there is reason to think that it is controlled by the central
nervous system.

Asserting that thinking is a central rather than a peripheral process
does not exclude the possibility that under certain circumstances peripheral
processes may interact with central processes, either facilitating them or in-
hibiting them. We have already seen (pp. 45–46) a clear example of this in the
case of the motor processes of speech; even though speech is controlled
centrally, that control appears to depend upon a continuous feedback of information from the periphery—both auditory and kinesthetic—and a disturbance of this feedback causes alterations in the kind of control exercised
centrally.

Another interesting case is that of the muscular movements that sometimes accompany silent reading. It has been shown [2] that mature, expert
readers can read even fairly difficult material without any detectable innerva-
tion of the speech musculature, but when the material becomes difficult
enough, they will start making subvocal movements of the tongue and lips,
as if subliminal speaking of the material will help them comprehend it. This
finding is also, possibly, evidence for the proposition that some forms of
mental activity develop through the gradual suppression of their overt
counterparts. According to some theoreticians, [3] "inner speech" (that is,
thinking which follows verbal patterns) develops in the child only in this way
—when it is no longer rewarding for the child to say everything aloud. On the
other hand, it is at least equally reasonable to assume that speech normally
originates as a total process involving *both* central and peripheral activity,
and that the child only gradually learns to suppress the peripheral component
when he so desires. This latter idea is the one to which I subscribe; it allows
us to assume that there can be some kind of mental content that is not
necessarily accompanied by speech activity. It makes more plausible, too, the
finding that prior to language acquisition children manifest cognitive activity
of considerable complexity—as in congenitally deaf children.

[2] Å. W. Edfeldt. *Silent speech and silent reading.* Chicago: University of Chicago
Press, 1960.
[3] L. S. Vygotsky. *Thought and language.* Cambridge and New York: M.I.T.-Wiley,
1962.

The Swiss psychologist Piaget and his associates have been responsible for an intense and protracted program of research on the development of thought in the child; their interest in the language development of the child has actually been secondary. Piaget distinguishes four main periods in the development of the child's thought, and since in their chief features his findings have been confirmed by other investigators, they deserve major emphasis here.

The average child in Western culture passes through the following stages of mental development:

acquisition of perceptual invariants:	to two years of age
preoperational intuitive thinking:	two to seven years of age
concrete operational thinking:	seven to eleven years of age
formal, propositional thinking:	eleven upwards

The ages given may be thought of as mental ages, in order to apply to children exhibiting different rates of development; of course, some hapless children never arrive at some of the later stages. The stages are cumulative; even in the stage of formal propositional thinking one is still acquiring perceptual invariants.

The first stage lays only the foundation for thought development. It is the stage during which, as we have already mentioned on page 35, the child learns to identify the main features of the world around him and some of their essential properties. He has to learn to perceive certain aspects of his environment as invariant despite the various forms in which they may appear; these *perceptual invariants* may be thought of as the basis of thought and language. The child learns the "meanings" of these percepts not only in terms of their direct sensory qualities but also in terms of the way objects and surfaces react to the various kinds of manipulative responses (touching, hitting, biting, and so on) that he finds he can make to them. Toward the end of this period the child has built covert, internalized, representational responses around these perceptual invariants, for he can delay his responses to a stimulus to a time when it is absent.

In the next stage of mental development distinguished by Piaget, the child wrestles with further problems in the interpretation of his environment, namely, the understanding of relationships among the perceptual invariants he has come to recognize. He must arrive at elementary concepts of space, time, and causality, but in so doing he remains for a considerable time in a "preoperational stage" in which he makes what Piaget calls intuitive judgments about relationships. For example, if the child is shown two rows of beads, each containing four beads but with one row spaced further apart than the other, he will in this stage consistently act and behave as if the more widely spaced row actually has more beads. Likewise, the child in this stage will maintain that a tall beaker, into which water from a low, wide beaker has been poured contains *more* water (or occasionally, *less* water) than was present when the self-same water was in the low wide beaker. The child

Cognition
and Thinking

has not arrived at a notion of the conservation of number or quantity. He attends to only one property of experience at a time, and cannot see how two or more properties (such as height and width) can interact or trade off with each other.

As a result of further learning through experience, the child eventually passes into the stage of "concrete operational thinking." He has acquired concepts involving complex relationships, such as that of the conservation of amount, weight, volume, size, and number, and has attained what Piaget calls *reversible* thinking—that is, thinking that can trace a physical operation back to its starting point and account for the transformations in its appearance. He can classify objects into groups of different sizes on the basis of different qualities; he can arrange objects in order of magnitude with respect to a given attribute, and he can perform such operations as substitution and the recognition of equivalences. But all his thought is bound to actual, tangible, visible materials and objects. He cannot at this stage imagine *possible*, potential relations among these objects, or manipulate possible relations among absent objects.

These latter capabilities develop, according to Piaget, only during the stage of formal, propositional thinking, that is, at around the start of adolescence for most children. It is during this stage that the child starts to think in terms of purely logical propositions which can be stated and tested against facts drawn from other experiences. This is the stage at which the child begins to be able to deal effectively with formally stated syllogisms.

Piaget and his associates have been principally concerned with describing the stages through which the child passes in development toward adult thinking. Their research program may be looked upon as a very elaborate testing enterprise, with an effort to understand the results noted in terms of a logical analysis and description of the mental operations or processes involved. They have made no attempt to investigate the possible effects of specific, deliberate tuition of mental processes, even though Piaget has insisted that mental development occurs only through processes of learning. Some American and British research has suggested, however, that although Piaget's stages are correct in their sequence, children's mental development can be hastened somewhat through specific teaching. For example, young children in the preoperational stage are, according to Piaget, incapable of identifying the shapes of alphabetical letters, but American research shows that this behavior can be produced in these children through appropriate schedules of discrimination training. Even though such accelerated learning can sometimes be effective, what the adult (and even the psychologist!) sometimes fails to appreciate is the large number of steps and the great variety of experiences that the child needs to go through in order to progress from one stage to another.

The unifying theme in the work of Piaget is the gradual unfolding of the individual's ability to construct an internal "model" of the universe around him and to perform manipulations on that model so as to draw conclusions about the probable past history of his environment or the probable results of possible actions that could be taken upon that environment. The ability to do this is the essence of all "thinking" in the nontrivial meanings of the term. The four stages of mental development listed by Piaget correspond to four stages in the working through of any process of thinking. The pre-thinking stage in which "perceptual invariants" are acquired by the infant corresponds to a stage of concept formation or concept attainment in which the basic entities which function in any particular context must be identified and recognized. The preoperational, intuitive stage may correspond to a type of "incubative" thought reported to occur even in adults when concepts involved in a problem are allowed to interact somewhat freely. The concrete operational stage corresponds to a stage when one experiments either overtly or covertly with the tangible referents of these concepts. The formal, propositional stage corresponds to the process of constructing alternative hypotheses regarding a problem, or linking together a series of inferences concerning a situation.

THE MOTIVATION OF THINKING

No process of thinking occurs without a cause. One class of causes is subsumed under the heading of motivation. In infancy, primary drives such as hunger, thirst, and the need for warmth provide a basis on which certain objects (such as foods, blankets) are discriminated, recognized, and built into concepts, but it is difficult to account for all the behavior of this period without also making reference to secondary, learned drives. In childhood, thinking is motivated not only by the need to solve problems concerned with the child's interactions with other people and with his environment, but also by a "need to understand" or to know, reinforced by experiences in which knowledge about the environment has been put to good use in solving problems of adjustment to it. Possibly this kind of motivation has its roots in the "orienting reflex," described by Russian psychologists as the primitive tendency noted in both animals and young children to pay attention to any novel stimulus.

Adults' thinking is also motivated, whether very diffusely, as in daydreaming and reverie, or very specifically, as when a particular problem urgently needs to be solved. An especially strong motivation for thinking arises from what Leon Festinger calls *cognitive dissonance*—a state of affairs that occurs whenever two ideas are in marked conflict, as when one is presented with an objective fact that appears to undercut one's cherished beliefs.[4] Festinger shows that people are strongly motivated to reduce such cognitive conflict—either by changing their attitudes, seeking more information, or restructuring or reinterpreting the information available to them.

In studying the motivation of thinking in problem-solving, the effect of instructional sets is noteworthy. The subject can be set to direct his thinking in a given way depending upon the task (German: *Aufgabe*) that he is given; this set has sometimes been called the "determining tendency." If a subject is given an *Aufgabe* to multiply the pairs of numbers given him, he will perform this task continuously whenever pairs of numbers are presented, but he can equally well be switched to a very different kind of response simply by

---

[4] L. Festinger. *A theory of cognitive dissonance.* New York: Harper & Row, 1957.

being told to add. Similar phenomena have been noted with controlled association tasks, as where the subject is given a series of directions like: "give the opposite of: SMALL . . . ; a superordinate of: CAT . . . ; a subordinate to: FOOD. . . . " It is as if the effect of the instruction is to program the subject to take a certain course of mental activity. The reader may notice the similarity of this kind of instruction to the programing effect which was claimed for a grammatical sentence in Chapter 4. A heard sentence is for a listener a kind of problem in thinking, and the effect of its grammatical structure is to induce sets for the responses to the stimuli referred to by the sentence.

CONCEPTS

Any analysis of thinking must accord an important role to what we call *concepts*. This term has cropped up in this book rather frequently, but we need to elaborate it still further.

The first concepts formed by the young child are the perceptual invariants of objects, sensations, sounds, and feelings that we have already mentioned. They are internal representations of classes or categories of experience. As the child learns language, he learns socially reinforced names for these categories of experience. He can even shape his behavior around internal representations of concepts; for example, a child at a certain age can take a pencil and draw a square on demand. Not all concepts can be overtly manifested in this way, of course, but a child who can correctly recognize instances of a particular concept and distinguish them from noninstances thereby demonstrates his acquisition of the concept.

Not all concepts are built out of raw sensations, either. Apparently some concepts are built out of partial similarities in the *responses* to sensations, and since some of these responses are internal, it is tempting to say that some concepts may be built out of other concepts. Take the concept of "oppositeness," which must be built out of instances in which it is noticed that one extreme of any dimension of sensation is contrasted with the other extreme. Similar analyses may be made for concepts like "number," "relation," or "randomness," whose genesis has been studied by Piaget. We can now broaden our definition of *concept* by asserting that any concept is the internal representation of a certain class of *experiences*, these experiences being either the direct response to aspects of the external environment, or responses to other experiences.

In theory, an infinite number of concepts are possible, since experiences may be classified in an infinity of ways. A concept can be arbitrarily constructed by combining other concepts: "All Colorado spruce trees between three and five feet in height situated on U. S. farms of 100 acres or more." But most concepts used in daily life, or in commerce, science, and the arts, are based on classifications of experience which have been found useful in some way. It has taken intelligence of a high order to make the first discovery and formulation of certain concepts like "gravitation," "relativity," "entropy," or, in the psychological sphere, "operant conditioning." These are indeed classifications of experience in the sense that there can be instances and noninstances of each of them; that they play a role in interpreting experience follows from our consideration of the use of concepts in thinking.

Concepts may vary in their degree of novelty and complexity for the individual. For an individual without considerable training in mathematics and physics, attaining a concept like that of *entropy* may be quite difficult because he may first have to attain an extensive series of prerequisite concepts. For a young child, attainment of the concept *oppositeness* may be equally difficult; he is unlikely to attain it until he has experienced oppositeness in a number of dimensions and notices a common pattern in these dimensions. On the other hand, many concepts may be very simple to acquire; often an individual can learn them by simply reading or hearing a verbal formulation of them; for example, the concept "card with two triangles and a red border" could probably be rather easily learned in this way by intelligent adult subjects. Most concepts an individual has to learn in school are of intermediate difficulty; usually the individual has to acquire them both by studying verbal formulations and practicing the recognition of instances and noninstances. The student of law or history, for example, will probably learn the concept *tort* in this way.

You must be careful to note what definition of concept learning is being used in a given instance. One definition has the virtue of complete objectivity; according to it, a person has learned a concept when he can with a high degree of reliability discriminate between instances and noninstances. This definition is usually satisfactory, but many individuals who know a concept by this definition are not able to formulate the concept verbally (or in whatever mode of communication is appropriate, for example, in visual or acoustic terms) or to communicate it to others. In fact, several experiments have shown, apparently, that it is possible to learn a concept without being aware of the basis for it; the individual simply learns a response to the significant features (that is, the "criterial attributes") of positive instances of a concept without being aware of this response. In one experiment,[5] Lorraine Bouthilet had subjects memorize a series of pairs, like *elephant-path* and *recognize-zero*. She then presented them with multiple-choice items like the following:

hexameter: (1) bib (2) tax (3) fat (4) get

Many subjects were able to choose the correct answer—*tax*—just on a "hunch," not realizing that the correct answer was always formed out of letters included in the stimulus word. Because such "unconscious" concept formation is possible, in some contexts, it is useful to define concept learning in terms of the ability to recognize instances *and* the ability to formulate descriptions, or to construct instances of the concept.

The role of verbal formulation in the attainment of concepts has been very little studied even though it is one of the prime methods of instruction used in schools. There is the danger of teaching merely parrot-like verbal formulations; William James, for example, recounts how some students were asked

[5] Lorraine Bouthilet. The measurement of intuitive thinking. Unpublished Ph.D. thesis, University of Chicago, 1948. Cited by R. Leeper, in S. S. Stevens (ed.). *Handbook of experimental psychology*. New York: Wiley, 1951, p. 745.

whether it would get warmer or colder as one dug a hole deeper and deeper into the earth; they could not reply, but prompted by their teacher they parroted the sentence "The interior of the globe is in a condition of igneous fusion."

Perhaps because of anecdotes like these (which do not really prove anything), the power of verbal formulation in teaching concepts has probably been underestimated. Verbal formulation should be valuable particularly when it is followed by copious presentation of positive and negative instances. A number of relevant experiments in the context of programed instruction indicate that the teaching of concepts can be accomplished by the presentation of "rules" and "examples," in that order, more effectively than by the presentation of examples *followed by* rules.

Extensive studies of concept attainment without the aid of externally supplied verbal formulations have been conducted by Heidbreder, Bruner, and others. Most of these experiments involve relatively simple combinatorial concepts utilizing dimensions of color, shape, number, and spatial position. Their basic design is to present subjects with a series of stimuli. The subject is told which stimuli exemplify, and which do not exemplify, the "concept," which the experimenter has decided on in advance. For example, in one of Edna Heidbreder's experiments the subject has to learn which pictures of an array are to be labelled with a particular nonsense syllable. Such experiments are more properly experiments in problem-solving, because the criterial attributes (things, forms, numbers, colors, and so on) are already well known to the subjects (usually college students). Nevertheless, it is of interest to study what processes occur in the course of a student's attainment of the solution.

Heidbreder's original notion that there is a natural order of concept attainment, in which concrete concepts (such as birds, faces) are more easily learned than abstract concepts (such as number and spatial position) seems to have been effectively disproved by evidence that the critical variable is the number of stimulus properties perceived by the subject.[6]

In conducting variations of this type of experiment, J. Bruner, J. Goodnow, and G. Austin [7] found that the ease of learning a concept was partly a function of its sheer complexity (the number of dimensions employed in it, and the like) and also of its logical structure; other things being equal, conjunctive concepts are easier than relational concepts; the most difficult of all are disjunctive concepts. A conjunctive concept is defined as one for which a specified combination of attributes is criterial (for example, "red figures with borders"); a disjunctive concept is one for which any of two or more alternative combinations of attributes is criterial ("either a red figure or one with 2 borders"); and a relational concept is one in which a specified relation between attributes is criterial ("fewer figures than borders").

Bruner and his associates were also interested in the "strategies" or "cognitive styles" adopted by their (college-age) subjects in solving the problems of concept attainment presented to them. These strategies, it should be borne in mind, apply to a situation in which the subject is shown a positive

6 For further details, consult S. A. Mednick. *Learning,* pp. 63–64, in this series.
7 J. Bruner, J. Goodnow, and G. Austin. *A study of thinking.* New York: Wiley, 1956.

instance of a concept and then asked to guess which other stimuli in an array are also positive instances; he is informed of the correctness of each successive guess. Four strategies were distinguished, as follows:

1. Simultaneous scanning: systematic trial of alternative hypotheses, with careful account taken of the information obtained from each success or failure.
2. Successive scanning: trial of one hypothesis at a time but without taking full advantage of the information supplied by successes and failures, so that some of the guesses are actually redundant or inconsistent.
3. Conservative focusing: trial of conservative variations of the selected focus or positive instance.
4. Focus gambling: drastic changes of focus, made in the hope of hitting on the criterial attributes by a process of elimination.

This kind of concept-formation experiment illustrates situations in which the individual develops and tests hypotheses (that is, "tentative" internal representations of experiences) concerning the concepts he is to acquire. Such behavior parallels, at a simple level, the behavior of the scientist seeking regularities in the phenomena he is studying.

There are, however, kinds of concept-attainment tasks where the concepts are so difficult or the attributes so lacking in salience that learning is gradual and hypotheses seem of no avail. In such cases, subjects find they must resort to "spectator behavior," simply waiting for the presentations to suggest suitable hypotheses.

Whatever the case may be, the most interesting object of study in these concept-formation experiments is how the individual arrives at hypotheses to test, for testing a hypothesis is itself relatively easy. Fast learners in these experiments are those who are facile in constructing hypotheses, either on account of some general trait (intelligence?) or on account of their previous acquisition of a rich variety of patterns of response likely to be useful in such experiments. Thus, transfer of prior learning ("learning to learn") can be effective in concept-attainment tasks.

PROBLEM-SOLVING
AS THE MANIPULATION OF CONCEPTS

During a lifetime, an individual acquires a goodly stock of concepts. He may also have acquired names (words or phrases) for many of these concepts, but it is not necessary for all concepts to have names. Some remain at a kinesthetic or perceptual level: For example, the concept of the lever is utilized by a farmer when he pries up a stone, even though he may not verbalize it with either of the words *lever* or *pry*. In such a case it might be thought that we could dispense with the notion of concept and assert that the response of the farmer is a direct learned response to a particular kind of problem, namely a stone which is hard to move. Nevertheless, the fact that the farmer may exhibit considerable planful behavior—going to get a crowbar, digging a socket for it, and finally moving it in a certain direction—

suggests that there is more than a direct overt response to the problem situation. On the other hand, the farmer might be hard pressed if someone asked him to explain how even a not-very-strong child can move, with a crowbar, a stone much heavier than himself.

All problem-solving—that is, thinking oriented toward the solution of problems—can be regarded as the manipulation of concepts that are evoked by the total situation and that may or may not be relevant to the task at hand. Depending on the nature of the situation, this manipulation may be at one extreme wholly internal, that is, not accompanied by detectable overt behavior, or at the other extreme, it may be almost wholly overt, directly involving relevant aspects of the environment. The former extreme would be exemplified in the solution of a numerical problem by a lightning calculator using mental arithmetic, the other extreme would be represented by the solution of a mechanical puzzle by manipulating it with guided trial and error. We must also recognize the utility of vicarious forms of interaction with the environment, such as making pencil sketches or physical models, solving mathematical equations on paper, or verbally formulating tentative conclusions. Among the factors that may determine whether an individual will solve a problem are the following:

1. The individual's repertoire of relevant concepts.
2. The concepts evoked in the individual by the structure of the problem.
3. The individual's skill in manipulating the concepts evoked, his strategy of solution, his flexibility in changing his mode of attack, and his ability to perceive the relevance of a concept.

These points can be illustrated by reference to what is probably the most famous series of experiments on problem-solving—Norman Maier's experiments with the "two-string problem." [8] A subject is introduced into a room with two pieces of string hanging from the ceiling and told that he is to tie their ends together; they are too far apart for him to reach both ends at once. The room is bare except for a chair, a piece of wire, and a pair of pliers. Several solutions of the problem are possible; one of them, however, seems to be particularly difficult for subjects to attain. This is the solution in which the end of one of the pieces of string is to be weighted with the pliers, set swinging, and caught after the subject has moved to grasp the end of the other string. The critical concept is that of a pendulum, and success usually follows as soon as the subject sees that he must make one of the strings into a pendulum. For many subjects, however, the situation does not evoke this concept readily; hanging strings are not perceived as potentially swinging, nor are the pliers perceived as a weight rather than as a tool. (The failure to see that an object can have a function other than its usual one has been called "functional fixedness.") However, A. J. Judson, C. N. Cofer, and S. Gelfand [9] found that subjects who have somehow been reminded of pendulums before being introduced to this problem (for example, by doing some memory work that involves the word *pendulum*) will tend to solve the

[8] N. R. F. Maier. *J. comp. Psychol.*, 1931, 12, 181–194.
[9] A. J. Judson, C. N. Cofer, and S. Gelfand. *Psychol. Repts.*, 1956, 2, 501–507.

problem more quickly than otherwise. Yet another technique for evoking the relevant concept, noted by Maier himself, is for the experimenter "accidentally" to brush against one of the strings, setting it swinging; in this case, however, the objective situation is changed so that it is more likely to evoke the relevant concept. Interestingly enough, in this latter case subjects are usually not even aware of the cue provided by the experimenter—a fact which casts suspicion on the dependability of subjects' verbal reports in studies of the thinking process.

We have discussed the cues to concepts provided by the problem or task itself, and the role of the individual's repertoire of concepts. But equally important is the way in which these concepts are manipulated in the process of arriving at solutions. Many problems require a sequential processing of concepts wherein each process yields some partial answer or tentative result to be subjected to still further processes, as, let us say, in long division. Factorial studies of individual differences in reasoning ability suggest that success in this kind of problem-solving partly depends on the individual's ability to retain these partial answers in short-term memory so that they are available for the next steps.

The steps themselves, of course, must be correct if the final solution is to be attained. Very often these steps take the form of inferences: *since A is the case, it follows that B; since B is the case, C follows;* and so on, when *A, B,* and *C* are propositions or statements of fact. The study of what kinds of inferences can properly be made from given propositions or premises is part of the domain of logic, a subject whose relations with psychology now must be considered.

LOGIC AND THE PSYCHOLOGY OF THINKING

The following problem was among a series presented to a number of college students who had no special training in logic:

> Mrs. Cooke had studied home economics in college. "Youth is a time of rapid growth and great demands on energy," she said. "Many youngsters don't get enough vitamins in their daily diet. And since some vitamin deficiencies are dangerous to health, it follows that the health of many of our youngsters is being endangered by inadequate diet." Does it follow that the health of many youngsters is being endangered by inadequate diet? Give your reasoning.

Mary Henle [10] reported that most of her subjects agreed with this reasoning. And most of these did so with no amplification beyond a restatement of the reasoning given by Mrs. Cooke. The well-known *fact* that inadequate diet is endangering the health of many youngsters seemed to influence the readiness of the subjects to endorse this reasoning. And yet some subjects must have had an intimation that the reasoning *as stated* was faulty. One said, "Correct, if we assume that the youngsters are lacking those vitamins in their diet which endanger health." Another said, "It seems to follow, assuming that the

[10] Mary Henle. *Psychol. Rev.*, 1962, 69, 366–378.

deficient vitamins are also the vital ones." We have no way of knowing how many subjects sensed the faulty reasoning but "corrected for it" by adding or assuming premises.

A great deal of the reasoning we do, and even the reasoning we see in newspapers, speeches, and the like, would not stand up under careful analysis from the standpoint of formal logic. Formal logic can be thought of as a branch of mathematics which enables one to test whether a stated conclusion validly follows from stated premises. The study of the syllogism is a kind of semantic analysis of the meanings of propositions using the words *all, some, not, and, or,* and several others (with carefully defined meanings) and the study of the degree to which sets of these propositions could be a consistent map or counterpart of selected aspects of the real world (or even an imaginary world). Textbooks of logic present various easily learned procedures for ascertaining the validity of inferences, and we shall not try to sketch them here.

Though logic and psychology are independent in a formal sense, the way we attempt to think logically—apart from training in formal logic—may be influenced by psychological processes which are worth studying.

In reasoning, we can use language to construct a "map" of a possible objective reality; the validity of the reasoning is perceived when the map is recognized as self-consistent. A simple reasoning process occurs when we have to figure out a satisfactory route between two isolated points in a city with whose general layout we are only vaguely familiar. We know how to get from A to B, and from C to D, say, but the question arises, does going to B take one too far out of the way to get easily to C and thence to D? Thinking out the route from B to C will help us perceive whether the whole plan is efficient. A somewhat analogous procedure is followed by a person trying to evaluate the validity of a reasoning process such as the one about vitamin deficiency; the verbal statement is a "program" for a construction of reality whose validity is to be tested. "Here are youngsters who don't get enough vitamins in their daily diet," a person could say. "And some vitamin deficiencies are dangerous to health. But are these 'dangerous' vitamin deficiencies included among the deficiencies asserted to occur in those youngsters? No, we are not told, so the conclusion doesn't necessarily follow." The "map" is not completely consistent. (The "Euler circles" and "Venn diagrams" presented in texts of formal logic are mechanical ways of translating syllogisms into "maps" and evaluating their consistency.)

In practice, as we have seen, people are likely to change or add premises to make the conclusions accord with their knowledge or belief. And people are distinctly troubled when they have to deal with premises stated abstractly or "nonsensically," as in the following:

All X are Y.	All skyscrapers are three-legged chairs.
Some Y are Z.	Some three-legged chairs fly.
Therefore, some X are Z.	Therefore, some skyscrapers fly.

In dealing with syllogisms presented formally, like these, people tend also to be influenced by what some investigators have called an "atmosphere effect": Affirmative premises create an atmosphere that tends to evoke acceptance of affirmative conclusions, regardless of the absolute logic of the matter.

Because the reasoning we do or experience in everyday life is so seldom stated in explicit syllogistic form, we are prone not to test its logical validity even if we can do so. Even courses in formal logic do not seem to produce startling changes in students' ability to spot faulty reasoning.

Faulty reasoning does not stem solely from failure to test syllogistic inferences. Frequently there is uncritical acceptance of premises, or the setting up of improper equivalences between terms. If it is asserted that "fluoridation of the water supply is a medication," it is necessary to know how people understand terms like "fluoridation" and "medication" before one can appraise the validity of the statement or use it in further reasoning.

Many of the effects of persuasive language arise through the use of words with emotionally toned connotative meanings. "Eagerness" and "aggressiveness" might properly be used to refer to the same kind of behavior, say, in a politician or an executive, but the former term has a higher position on the semantic differential Evaluative Scale (p. 103) and is thus more likely to arouse favorable attitudes toward the person to whom it is applied.

A wryly delightful example of the skillful use of connotative meanings to suppress the evocation of undesirable emotional attitudes is the language of undertakers, as reported by Jessica Mitford in *The American Way of Death*. Instead of the *body* or the *corpse*, they use the name of the deceased: Mr. Jones, or Mrs. Smith, or whatever, thus arousing the responses that had been made to the *living* person. They do not speak of digging and filling a grave, but of *opening* and *closing* it. The *person* (not the body) is *interred* rather than buried, not in a cemetery or graveyard but in a *memorial park*. The word *death* is avoided at all costs: A death certificate is a *vital statistics form*, and the deceased didn't die, but *expired*.

Language and Cognition

Even though, as we have seen in Chapter 6, many kinds of thinking are possible without language, language can obviously play a large role in thinking—a role that will be explored in this chapter. Among the ideas that we shall want to examine are these: that language may facilitate thinking, allowing it to be more complex, efficient, and accurate; that language may in some cases inhibit or misguide thinking; and that the structure of a particular language may channel thinking and thus cause the users of that language to think either more or less efficiently and accurately than they would if they were to use another language, or even to arrive at

89

7

different conclusions or different solutions to problems from what speakers of the other language would do.

In the last chapter we studied the processes by which both animals and children acquire concepts; we defined a concept as an internal representation of a class of experiences. We saw that many concepts are acquired without language.

What is the relation of language responses to these concepts? It is possible, of course, for a child to learn a language response without an underlying concept—he may learn simply to echo a word, without understanding it, or he may use it in an inappropriate context. But learning to use a word in a meaningful way—that is, using it in such a way that it will be consistently socially reinforced—implies that the child has acquired the concept which underlies the linguistic response. The child who can use the word *ball* for the same class of experiences the members of his speech community do has, we may say, acquired a concept called *ball*, and he will use this word when he encounters new instances. If he shows any tendency to overgeneralize the concept—say, to call a strawberry a ball—he will be corrected. If he undergeneralizes the concept—that is, fails to apply it to certain experiences—the tendency will probably be corrected when others use it for that class of experience.

One function of linguistic forms is to provide a cue for the formation of a new concept. The adult who tells a child that there is such a thing as a platypus, for example, alerts the child to the existence of a possible class of experiences; pictures and descriptions of platypuses then help the child to fix the boundaries of this class of experiences. Perhaps the child will never actually see a live platypus. Even the word *unicorn* is a name for a *possible* class of experiences and the child who learns this concept would at least be able to identify a unicorn if one ever presented itself! Some concepts are explicitly imaginary, like $i = \sqrt{-1}$ in mathematics; they refer to a conceivable and useful class of experiences that will, it is known, never occur in reality.

One characteristic of a language that can be used in general communication (whether it is "natural," like English or Chinese, or "artificial," like Esperanto or Basic English) is that it provides words or linguistic forms sufficient to catalog or describe all or nearly all the experiences or classes of experience that occur to the user of the language. Of course, languages vary in the sizes of their vocabularies; the vocabulary size of a language is chiefly a function of the state of advancement of the civilization which underlies it. But the "core vocabularies"—that is, the vocabularies of everyday parlance and general use in writing—of all languages are of roughly the same order of magnitude, say, somewhere around 10,000 words, and furthermore, they show a surprising degree of correspondence. That is to say, the speakers of the world's languages agree to a considerable extent on the concepts they have found convenient to symbolize with words. To a large degree, this is because of certain uniformities in the physical and biological environments of mankind: *sun, moon, water, fire, stone, flower, bug* are names of physical or biological entities found nearly everywhere, and in nearly every language there is one principal linguistic form for symbolizing them. In Helen Eaton's *Semantic Frequency List for English, French, German, and Spanish,* 662 concepts are listed that in each of these four languages have words occurring in the first thousand words in order of frequency; this list starts off (in English) with the "concepts" *a, able, about* (concerning), *about* (approximately), be *about* to, *above.* In Basic English, an essentially artificial language based on English, developed by C. K. Ogden, it is possible to express any nontechnical idea within a vocabulary of only 850 words.

In Chapter 2 we stressed that a language is made up not only of words, but also of other linguistic forms both smaller and larger than words, and of constructions. It seems reasonable to suppose that each linguistic form and construction symbolizes a concept as we have defined it: an internal representation of a (possible) class of experiences. This leads us to examine the kinds of concepts symbolized in language. The form-class "allegiances" of linguistic forms have a very interesting relevance here: On the one hand, linguistic forms are learned *as* members of form-classes because of their positions in constructions; since they are experienced in this way a form-class is itself a concept (a class of experiences). On the other hand, the concepts contained in a form-class *themselves* represent experiences which may tend to have common elements among themselves and hence may tend to form a class. These two tendencies result in the investing of a form-class with a certain "meaning." For example, the form-class of transitive verbs which includes *hit, kill, throw, drop,* and other physical actions also includes the verbs *have* and *owe,* which therefore may tend to absorb a meaning of "physical action" because they are classified with physical actions.

We can return, then, to the analysis of linguistic form-classes in Chapter 2. What we there called meanings are now to be called concepts—internal representations of classes of experiences. For speakers of English, we can postulate the broad organization of major form-class concepts shown in Table 4. These classes very nearly exhaust the conceptual structure on which English form-classes are based: Linguistic forms that do not fit clearly into any of these form classes are chiefly items that perform miscellaneous functions in the mechanism of the grammar—mostly, they are signs or markers of form-classes or of constructions, or directions for interpreting a certain construction.

The constructions listed on page 20 can also be postulated to correspond to concepts or classes of experience, and the meanings given there can be taken to be approximate descriptions of those classes of experience. These particular constructions are the patterns for complete utterances; the underlying class of experiences they symbolize therefore include the communication situations in which these constructions are used. For example, the subject-predicate construction which underlies the sentence *Jim saw Bob* represents not only that class of experiences in which something is asserted about a nominal (Jim, in this case), but also that class of experiences in which information is furnished to a hearer (rather than being requested of him).

Many of the concepts of language are learned without the learner's being aware of them. This is true of most grammatical concepts. Even though these

TABLE 4

Major Form-Class Concepts

Class	Linguistic Manifestation *	Approximate Conceptual Meaning— The Class of Experiences That Includes:
Nominals	Nouns, pronouns, noun phrases	Objects, persons, ideas, and relations whose location or distribution in space, actually or metaphorically, can be specified
Adjectivals	Adjectives, adjective phrases	Qualities or attributes perceived as applying to nominals, either on an all-or-none basis (presence-absence) or in terms of degree
Verbals	Verbs, verb phrases	Events, relationships, or states whose location or distribution in a time dimension can be specified
Adverbials	Adverbs, adverb phrases	Qualities or attributes perceived as applying to adjectivals and verbals, either on an all-or-none basis or in terms of degree
Prepositionals	Prepositions, prepositional phrases	Relations of spatial, temporal, or logical position relative to nominals
Conjunctives	Conjunctions	Logical relations occurring whenever any two or more members of any class (or construction) are considered together

* In each case it is to be understood that derivations from other form classes are to be included.

concepts refer to certain classes of experience, many people never become aware of these classes. If presented with two sentences with partially similar structure, many people have difficulty in identifying the analogous parts. For example, what word in the second sentence has the same grammatical function as *him* in the first sentence?

We showed him the way to get there.
He wanted to buy his mother a present.

Some constructions, in fact, carry concepts that often seem to be hard to attain on a conscious level. For example, the construction *the X-er . . ., the Y-er . . .* (as exemplified in *the faster I ran the better I felt*) carries the concept of correlation, which is sometimes hard for beginning students of statistics to grasp. These same students can often be helped by referring to this linguistic construction and its meaning.

It is probably at this point—that is, the grammatical construction—that language structure begins to be of real help in aiding thinking beyond what could happen without language. By means of grammatical constructions one can learn, remember, and manipulate more complex concepts, such as:

the boy's hat
herbivorous mammals
the top of the Rock of Gibraltar
preoccupation with litigation
excess of income over outgo
psychologists aroused over ethical problems
two right turns after each left turn

Thinking aided by language is called *reasoning*, and the ability to reason depends largely on the ability to formulate steps in an inferential process in terms of language. An interesting question is, how complete and "grammatical" does such a formulation have to be? It is hard to get evidence on this question, for reasoning usually occurs internally. There have been attempts to observe these internal processes by the method of *réflexion parlée* (French for "spoken thinking"), in which the individual is asked to "talk aloud" his reasoning processes. There can be no guarantee, of course, that the subject can give a full verbalization of his reasoning processes, even with every intention of doing so. Furthermore, it is possible that the very process of producing an overt verbalization affects the course of the reasoning process; one study found that committing thought to writing too quickly delays its full development, and the same thing may easily be true of "spoken thinking." In fact, most verbal reports obtained by this method seem to be just that: reports of *something that has already happened*. The speaking a subject does in the course of solving a reasoning problem does not seem to be identical with reasoning processes but instead a rather inaccurate and hazy report of them. It is thus difficult to obtain evidence on the proposition enunciated earlier in this paragraph—that the ability to reason depends on verbally formulated inferential steps. Nevertheless, the content of reasoning processes frequently can be stated only in verbal terms, even though the end result of a reasoning process may be an action, such as a decision to buy an automobile.

THE ROLE OF LANGUAGE IN COGNITIVE DEVELOPMENT

Animals can perform many tasks that appear to require "thinking" or at least some internal process which is not immediately open to observation. For example, an adult monkey can be trained to perform the "double alternation problem"—that is, to learn that, in a sequence of trials in which he can look for food under either a box at the right (R) or a box at the left (L), the sequence which will always get him food is RRLLRRLL. . . . Some kind of symbolic activity appears to be involved because the monkey has to remember, or keep track of, whether he has looked under a given box before. We cannot say whether the monkey "counts" in any sense; all we can really know is whether he can learn to perform the task.

One of the favorite strategies of psychologists in studying the mental development of young children is to give them some of the same problems that they give animals. That is, a child is introduced into a situation analogous to what might be presented to a rat or a monkey; while the experimenter may talk to the child, he will talk only in general terms (saying something like "We're going to play a new game") and will studiously avoid telling the child what the experiment is about or what rules are to be followed. The advantage of this procedure is that it allows the experimenter to study the speed and accuracy with which the child can "figure out" for himself the rules or principles of the experiment; there is much interest and merit in this approach. Unfortunately, experimenters have only rarely taken the additional step of seeing whether their young subjects could also be taught the principles of the experiment solely by verbal instruction. For example, the double alternation problem described above has been tried with children. It has been found that they cannot learn to perform it until they are about three-and-a-half years old at the youngest, and from that age until about the age of five, they cannot verbalize the rule by which they perform it. By the age of five, most normal children can both learn the task and verbalize it. There is no systematically collected information about how early children can be taught the double alternation problem by verbal instruction alone.

It seems obvious, however, that if a child has already learned a concept *verbally* in the course of his everyday development, he would be more likely to perform successfully in any problem situation where this concept is critical, even though it does not figure explicitly. This conclusion is supported by a number of experiments. C. C. Spiker, I. R. Gerjuoy, and W. O. Shepard tested a group of children aged three to five and divided them into those who could say something like "middle-sized" as the way to describe the middle-sized member of a series of three stimuli, and those who could not.[1] This capability was then found to be highly correlated with the child's performance in a concept-attainment experiment where it was necessary to choose the middle-sized stimulus from sets of three stimuli in which the absolute sizes of the stimuli varied. (When the absolute size of the middle-sized stimulus was constant, prior learning of the concept "middle-sized" turned out to be irrelevant because the children could learn to respond to the absolute size of the critical stimulus.) It should be noted, incidentally, that the training period of the experiment itself was too short to allow learning of the concept of middle-sized-ness in the case of children who had not acquired it before. Apparently, learning a concept of this complexity is something that takes a considerable amount of time; probably it depends on a variety of other learnings that would have to be explicitly provided for if it were to be taught in an experimental setting.

There has been much interest in the question of whether language responses help or hinder nonverbal behavior in ways that go beyond the ones indicated above. Does having names for stimuli help one respond differentially to them? Does it help one remember them, or use them in further problems? This question has now been investigated fairly extensively, both with children and adults, although the answers we have are not always clear or convincing, and we have no settled theory to explain the results.

One thing seems clear: Having names for things does not alter our ab-

---

[1] C. C. Spiker, I. R. Gerjuoy, and W. O. Shepard. *J. comp. physiol. Psychol.*, 1956, 49, 416–419.

solute capacity to discriminate among these things when they are extremely similar. Perhaps you have heard that workers in dye factories learn many more names for colors and hence become better able to discriminate colors. The latter part of this statement is not quite true, if by "discrimination" we mean the ability to detect a small difference between two stimuli when they are juxtaposed, as in a psychophysical experiment. Highly skilled workers in occupations dealing with color or taste or any other sensory dimension are on the average no better able to make psychophysical discriminations than the average person (unless they have been selected for sensory ability in the first place). But the special names they learn for colors *do* help in one way: They facilitate communication, and, what is more interesting for the present discussion, they enhance the ability of people to recognize and identify particular hues from memory. This has been demonstrated by R. W. Brown and E. H. Lenneberg in an experiment with American college women.[2] In one part of their experiment, they established that a series of colors differed in what they called *codability*. Highly codable colors were those which the women named easily and promptly, and for which there was high agreement on names. In the second part of their experiment, they showed that the codability of a color was significantly related to how well it could be recognized in a task such as the following: A subject was shown four colors simultaneously for three seconds; then after a half minute she had to find these colors in a large chart containing 120 colors systematically arranged. When the subjects were asked how they performed this task, they reported that they named the colors to themselves while the colors were exposed, and then used the names they remembered in finding the colors on the large chart.

The advantage of words in various sorts of tasks in which perceived impressions have to be "stored" and remembered in some way has been demonstrated in numerous experiments. Sometimes the words are ones that the individual has already learned in his language in the normal course of experience (as in the Brown and Lenneberg experiment); sometimes they are words or nonsense syllables whose meanings are learned in the initial phases of the experiment. The superior potency of a *word* as a carrier of a sense impression is revealed even when an experiment is designed so that an equal amount of attention is paid to the stimuli during initial learning. K. H. Kurtz and C. I. Hovland [3] had one group of children circle on a sheet of paper the *words* that went with a series of objects being shown to them, while another group circled *pictures* of these objects. One week later, the first group of children were better able than the second group to recall or recognize the objects that had been shown. Also, the possibility of modifying the learning of subjects by varying the "meaning" of words or other verbal responses has been clearly shown in various experiments. If two different objects (or stimuli) are assigned the same name by the experimenter, the two objects are more likely to be responded to in the same way than if the objects are given different names. Winifred Shepard [4] found that teaching a child to call a series of red, orange, and yellow lights by the same nonsense-syllable

[2] R. W. Brown and E. H. Lenneberg. *J. abnorm. soc. Psychol.,* 1954, 49, 454–462.
[3] K. H. Kurtz and C. I. Hovland. *J. exp. Psychol.,* 1953, 45, 157–164.
[4] W. O. Shepard. *Child Devt.,* 1956, 27, 173–178.

names will cause him to generalize a button-pushing response to all these lights even though the original training was only to the red light.

If, as appears above, words assigned to stimuli can modify an individual's responses to those stimuli, it is possible that the individual can be deceived by these labels, or at least, have his responses changed in ways that are not completely what he might desire if he were aware of them. This fact is the basis of certain semantic fallacies to which we are prone. S. I. Hayakawa pointed out many years ago that if a certain kind of payment to the unemployed was called "social insurance benefits" it was likely to be perceived favorably, whereas if it was labelled "relief" it was likely to be perceived unfavorably. Let's look, however, at experimental evidence on how verbal labels can sometimes deceive a person.

A classic experiment on this problem was done by L. Carmichael, H. P. Hogan, and A. A. Walter. They found that when subjects were briefly exposed to the figures shown in Figure 12, and later asked to reproduce them, the reproductions were influenced by the labels assigned to the figures at the time of original exposure. For example, the ◯–◯ tended to be reproduced as something like ◯◯ if it had been labelled "eyeglasses" whereas it might be reproduced ◯–◯ if it had been labelled "dumbbells." Further experi-

Word list I	Stimulus figures	Word list II
Bottle		Stirrup
Crescent moon		Letter "C"
Beehive		Hat
Eyeglasses		Dumbbells
Ship's wheel		Sun
Gun		Broom
Two		Eight

Figure 12. Figures used by Carmichael, Hogan, and Walter in their experiment on the influence of language on perception. To one group of subjects, the stimulus figures were presented labelled with the words of Word List I, and to another group of subjects with the words of Word List II. (Adapted from L. Carmichael et al. J. exp. Psychol., 1932, 15, 73–86.)

mental analyses of this phenomenon [5] support the conclusion that the label presented by the experimenter tends to "channel" the stimulus function of the figure in the direction of the concept represented by the label; unless the subject has prolonged opportunity to study the figure, or the delay period is relatively short, it is principally this "concept" that is remembered, rather than some direct representation. Indeed, even subjects who are not shown any verbal label will invent their own labels and their later reproductions of the figures will often reveal the nature of these labels. It should be noted, incidentally, that the use of a label, whether by the subject alone or also by the experimenter implies that the label refers to a concept; thus, the figure is perceived as being one of a class of similar experiences named by the concept.

A label is not particularly useful when it does not readily refer to a well-learned class of experiences. For example, efforts by several experimenters to teach people to recognize novel visual patterns better by assigning nonsense syllables to them have not been successful. There is, in fact, a series of experiments which purport to demonstrate that stimuli can "acquire distinctiveness" *solely* by having verbal responses attached to them. The theory is that when a verbal tag has been attached to a stimulus, the implicit responses to that verbal tag enhance the total discriminability of the stimulus in relation to other stimuli. Actually, there is no good evidence for any such effect. The experiments show only that words themselves are discriminable to varying degrees, or that subjects make varying use of words in mediating discriminations; these conclusions have been reached also through other types of experiments.

An experiment conducted by Kathryn Norcross has sometimes been cited as evidence for the "acquired distinctiveness of stimuli." [6] She taught children the names *zim* and *zam* for the faces in one pair, and the names *wug* and *kos* for the faces in another pair. Later she had the children learn a motor response (pushing a particular button) for each face, and found that the responses were less easily learned to similarly named faces (*zim, zam*) than to dissimilarly named faces (*wug, kos*). But since her procedure called for the child to say the correct name for each face before making his motor response, her experiment may be regarded as showing merely that it is harder to learn associations to relatively similar verbal stimuli than to dissimilar verbal stimuli—a conclusion which has been repeatedly demonstrated in verbal paired-associates experiments. It is difficult to conceive of an experimental design for demonstrating "acquired distinctiveness of stimuli" that will not be subject to the criticism that the discrimination is made in response to words, or more generally, verbal mediation, rather than to characteristics of the stimuli that are somehow invested in them by the words assigned to them. The hypothesis that discrimination responses can be made to verbal mediators is interesting enough in itself, and seems a more reasonable interpretation of the experimental facts.

People vary in the degree to which they notice and concern themselves with the various kinds of attributes that characterize the things and events

[5] D. T. Herman, R. H. Lawless, and R. W. Marshall. *Percept. Motor Skills,* 1957, 7, *Monog. Suppl.* 2, 171–186.

[6] K. J. Norcross. *J. exp. Psychol.,* 1958, 56, 305–309.

of the environment. A forester will be more ready than the average person to notice differences among various kinds of trees. A machinist would more readily notice the difference between right-handed and left-handed bolts than the ordinary household do-it-yourselfer would. Obviously, these differences in response-tendency come about through learning, but there is evidence that language can play a special role in this learning. The very existence of contrasting words for different categories or for different values of a dimension draws attention to these categories or values, and if a person has to learn to use these words in a way that is acceptable in his speech community, he must of necessity notice and discriminate the corresponding stimuli. The effect of language is thus to make the differences among stimuli more noticeable, or salient, than they would otherwise be. Evidence for this effect comes from a cross-linguistic experiment described on pp. 108–109.

The important role of verbal mediators in behavior is so well attested that it can hardly be denied. It supplies a ready explanation, too, for many otherwise incomprehensible changes in behavior as a child matures. In his early years, the child's responses to his environment tend to be direct—the outcome of *immediate* connections that have been learned between stimuli (or classes of stimuli, for stimulus generalization occurs very early) and responses, either by classical or by operant conditioning. As the child attains concepts which he can retain and respond to internally, he is able to respond to the environment in an indirect, less immediate manner. For example, at some point in a child's development he can be taught to identify the larger of two stimuli no matter what their absolute sizes may be, whereas at an earlier stage he can respond only in terms of absolute sizes. He is presumably responding in terms of a concept rather than in terms of direct perceptions of stimuli. Some psychologists have thought that the changeover from direct to mediating-response behavior takes place at one particular stage, perhaps about the time the child begins to solidify his use of language. Examination of the total array of pertinent experimental literature suggests, however, that this changeover is a gradual process; each particular concept is, to be sure, learned more or less once and for all, but concepts vary widely in difficulty and in the time required to learn them, and hence also in the age of the child when they are likely to be learned. In fact, some concepts are not learned until relatively late in life by some people. If the learning of a concept is accompanied by the learning of a particular verbal response, the potency of the concept in behavior is likely to be enhanced; concept learning is more likely to be accompanied by overt verbal learning, the older the individual is.

One other striking effect of the development of verbal mediators lies in making the individual better able to state and test hypotheses. In fact, this trend seems to be highly correlated with mental development as a whole as measured by mental tests. Interesting evidence for this was obtained, ironically enough, in an experiment in which it was shown that high-IQ children were *less* successful than children of average IQ in solving certain kinds of problems in which many irrelevant stimuli were present.[7] Apparently, the high-IQ children were hampered because they spent time developing and testing hypotheses concerning the irrelevant stimuli, whereas the children of average

[7] S. F. Osler and G. E. Trautman. *J. exp. Psychol.*, 1961, 62, 9–13.

IQ learned which stimuli were relevant by simple associational learning processes.

We have plenty of evidence for inferring the existence of concepts and other mediating processes by noting that some such processes must function in experiments of the sort we have been describing. The question now is, can we study these processes *for themselves?* Can we describe them more completely and get at their fundamental nature?

We shall describe and discuss a number of different methods that have been devised. Each method involves the eliciting of certain kinds of overt, objective responses from which reasonable inferences about the nature of the underlying mediating processes may be drawn. Each method yields interesting and suggestive evidence, but no one method can give the whole answer we want.

Free Association

The free association experiment has already been introduced in Chapter 4 as a way of showing that verbal behavior is fairly predictable. The responses given by a person to a verbal stimulus in the free association experiment are presumably mediated by the concept this stimulus evokes and hence give evidence of the nature of this concept. A person who is presented with an ambiguous stimulus like *LIGHT* and asked to give a series of associations to it will generally give either a series like *heavy, feather, weight,* and so on, or a series like *dark, color, white;* he will rarely switch from one concept to the other.

The free association experiment is quite sensitive to the influence of set. It is perceived by people as a particular kind of task; that is to say, "thinking of the first word that comes to mind" means different things to different people. To young children it often tends to mean "think of the next word you would use in a sentence," so that to the stimulus *LIGHT* a child might give the response *bulb* (light-bulb). To adults, it is more likely to mean, "think of another word in the same part of speech as the stimulus and with a partially similar meaning." To some adults, it seems to mean, "think of a word that *contrasts* in meaning with the stimulus as much as possible." The different sets with which people approach the free association task and the effects of these sets have not yet been adequately studied. We do, however, have extensive compilations of the frequency of responses to standard stimulus lists in representative American populations; they give evidence of the nature of certain concepts in these populations. Here, for example, is a list of all the words given in response to the stimulus *LIGHT*, and their frequencies, in a sample of 1008 college students:[8]

[8] From W. A. Russell and J. J. Jenkins. *The complete Minnesota norms for responses to 100 words from the Kent-Rosanoff Word Association Test.* University of Minnesota, Department of Psychology, 1954.

647 dark
78 lamp
30 bright
25 sun
23 bulb
16 heavy, day
12 house
11 see
10 window
5 switch, soft,
  candle, black,
  heat, darkness,
  white
4 night

3 shade(s), red, brightness, yellow, heaven,
  color, weight
2 shadow, street, health, green, hair, electric,
  blue, morning, match, clear
1 look, shine, high, out, glass, electricity,
  awaken, star, sky, cheery, read, warm, sunshine,
  spot, club, feather, object, brown, electric
  bulb, hand, Edison, sound, hard, study, dark or
  heavy, waves, apple, path, air, luminous, beam,
  time, post, fair, flame, lamb, eyes, dirt,
  easy, creamy, hurts eyes, love, world, lift,
  desert, snow, lightning, year, truth, ceiling,
  boat, daytime, earth, beach, glow, head

The frequency distribution somewhat resembles the frequency distribution of all the words in large general samples of English text; in fact, Davis Howes [9] has pointed out that the summed frequencies of all the words obtained in free association responses are highly correlated with the frequencies of those words in English in general; he therefore regards the word association test as little more than a special way of "tapping into" a person's total repertoire of responses. This does not explain, however, how the particular associates of a word get to be selected.

Probably the best way of explaining word association responses is to assume that a stimulus evokes some part of the concept named by the stimulus, that is, some part of an assemblage of mediating processes. Exactly what parts of this assemblage will be evoked depends on the set with which the individual approaches the task and on other factors. The overt response is then a name elicited by the particular fraction of the mediating response evoked. In order to give a series of associations to the same stimulus, an individual may have to change his set slightly, or deliberately "think of" the stimulus in different ways. He usually exhausts the most immediate and "obvious" associations in the first few seconds of the response period; the more remote associations take much longer. Generally, the word association test is given in such a way as to require only one or a small number of responses to each stimulus; analysis of data is based on the responses of large numbers of people. The results are thus not only a function of what aspects of a given concept are most frequently found in a group, but also of what "sets" are most likely to be adopted by the respondents. If we analyze the results given above for *LIGHT*, it would seem that only about 2.2 per cent of the sample interpreted the word as the opposite of *heavy*, while most of the rest interpreted it either as the opposite of *dark*, or as a noun. Further, a majority of each group approached the word with an "oppositeness" set to give words like *dark, heavy,* and other "contrast" words.

There have been some elaborate attempts to infer from free association data the concepts underlying the stimuli and responses. All that we can say here is that the data support the notion that most concepts contain, as it were, a cluster of attributes which have been experienced by the individual

[9] D. Howes, *J. abnorm. soc. Psychol.,* 1957, 54, 75–85.

in association with the concept. For example, the concept underlying the word (railroad) *train* may contain representations of other concepts like *fast, powerful, hard, dangerous,* and *boring,* depending on the experiences of the individual with trains. Not all of these attributes are criterial, of course; in fact, few of them are. The task of stating exactly what a *train* is, is a far cry from the task of giving "free associations" to the word *train*.

Be that as it may, the results of word association compilations are of great use in predicting the outcomes of various kinds of experiments involving words. For example, it is much harder to learn pairs of words selected at random than it is to learn pairs of words that are frequently given to each other as associations, or that give the same sets of associations (for example, *MAN* and *GIRL* are seldom given as associates of each other, but in common yield the association *WOMAN*). Also, word association results can predict the outcomes of verbal experiments in transfer of training: If one learns a pair A-B, it is then easier to learn the pair A-C if B and C are associates according to free association data.

We have already mentioned (page 41) the use of free association procedures to define what has been called *meaningfulness*. The number of different associations that a stimulus elicits in a person in a certain period of time, say one minute, gives a measure that, when averaged over a representative sample of respondents, will very well predict the ease of learning to pair that stimulus with another stimulus. This measure of meaningfulness can be applied either to real words or to nonsense syllables. Meaningfulness, measured in this way, can be interpreted as an index of the variety of experiences represented in a concept, and learning is facilitated when there are a variety of associated experiences with which to form connections.

When a subject responds to *BUTTERFLY* with the word *MOTH,* is it because there is a "direct," immediate connection between the words, or is it because the individual "thinks of" a butterfly, possibly even evokes an image of it, and then names an object similar to a butterfly? We have no good way of answering this question at present, which amounts to saying that the data can be explained on either basis. The most parsimonious interpretation is to assume that all associations are direct and immediate, pure responses to stimuli. It would even seem that associations form a sort of network in the mind, and that the results of experiments in verbal learning are most easily accounted for by noting how far away on the network any two words are in terms of free association data. Operationally, such an interpretation may be in order, but it seems a little too pat. A more reasonable interpretation is that the associations between words reflect the extent to which the underlying concepts share representations of attributes or related experiences. Consider the remarkable experiment of W. A. Russell and L. H. Storms,[10] who found that their results could be predicted very well solely from the norms for free association responses. What they found was that if a student first learned a pair like *DAX-WAR,* he could later learn a new response for *DAX, JUSTICE,* better than if he had not earlier learned *DAX-WAR*. The relevance of free association norms is this: A highly popular response to *WAR* is *PEACE* (but almost never *JUSTICE*), and a highly

[10] W. A. Russell and L. H. Storms. *J. exp. Psychol.,* 1955, 49, 287–293.

popular response to *PEACE* is *JUSTICE*. The results tempt one to conclude that the transfer of learning operates by relying on a chain of association bonds, *WAR* → (*PEACE*) → *JUSTICE*, without any reference to the meanings of these words. But an alternative hypothesis is possible and has not been checked: that subjects construct a reason for associating *WAR* and *JUSTICE* on the basis of their meanings (for instance, "a just war is one fought for justice"), and that such constructions are more likely to occur to the subject in the case of words that the experimenter has paired because the association nouns allow him to regard their associations as chained.

Osgood's "Semantic Differential" Technique

Charles Osgood, a psychologist who has been one of those chiefly responsible for developing the theory of the verbal mediator, took the bold step of deciding to get subjects to report directly on the nature of their concepts. But instead of asking them an open-ended question like "What is your concept of X?", he devised an ingenious method adapted from rating-scale procedures. He asked his subjects to *rate* their concepts on a series of scales.[11]

Let us digress a moment to consider the psychological basis of the process of rating. Suppose we take any two words at random, say *tree* and *stone*, and ask a group of people to indicate in what respects these concepts differ, as indeed they must. Among some of the answers we are likely to get are these: A tree is *alive*, while a stone is *inert*; a tree is relatively *flexible*, a stone is *rigid*. That is to say, the mention of any two concepts evokes a series of perceptual or conceptual dimensions in which they differ. Furthermore, many of these dimensions are recognized to exist in varying degrees. Therefore, it is possible to ask a subject to conceive the dimensions as represented by a straight line and to assign concepts positions on this line. For example, on the dimension flexible-rigid, I might assign *tree* and *stone* positions as follows:

because in my experience stones have been about as rigid as anything can be, whereas trees tend to be somewhat flexible, but not very much so—not so much, say, as a rubber band. Note that these are solely probabilistic statements; certainly some kinds of trees are much more flexible than others, and some kinds of "stone" (sheets of mica, for example) are somewhat flexible. They merely express my "average" concepts of tree and stone.

It is evident that to get a fully rounded idea of my concepts of tree and stone, an investigator would have to get ratings of them on a large variety of dimensions. How many dimensions, indeed, would be needed? In working out an answer to this question, Osgood collected 50 dimensions named by different pairs of adjectives and then resorted to the statistical technique of factor analysis (see page 67) to see whether this list of dimensions, or

[11] C. E. Osgood, G. J. Suci, and P. H. Tannenbaum. *The measurement of meaning.* Urbana: University of Illinois Press, 1957.

scales, could be pared down to a relatively small number of "basic" dimensions. This required the collection of data from a large group of respondents (as usual, college students) who rated 20 different concepts on the 50 scales. The somewhat unexpected result was that the 50 dimensions reduced themselves to three basic dimensions, or "factors":

1. Dimensions like good-bad, pleasant-unpleasant, sacred-profane, reduce themselves to what Osgood called an *Evaluation* factor, because the ratings of concepts on all these dimensions tended to be intercorrelated.
2. Similarly, dimensions like strong-weak, large-small, and heavy-light reduced themselves to what was called a *Potency* factor.
3. Finally, dimensions like active-passive, fast-slow, and sharp-dull reduced themselves to a basic *Activity* factor.

Now, it is obvious that these three factors are not the only independent dimensions by which concepts can be described. For example, stories can be rated along the dimension serious-humorous, a dimension which is largely independent of any of the three dimensions listed above. Nevertheless, repeated studies in a variety of cultures and with different sets of scales and concepts have rather consistently pointed to these three dimensions as the ones that apply to concepts most generally and most saliently.[12]

This is an important result, one that we must pause to consider rather thoroughly. It suggests that three important aspects of any "concept" correspond to its positions on the three basic dimensions indicated—how "good," how "strong," and how "active" it is perceived to be. Few concepts are neutral on all three of these scales. The evaluative scale is intimately connected with a basic psychological process: the satisfying, rewarding, or reinforcing property of a stimulus (or conversely, the displeasing, punishing, or nonreinforcing property of a stimulus). Thus, one's concept of any class of stimuli includes an assessment of its average reward value—either to oneself or to the society with which one identifies. The potency scale is probably connected with our perceptions of the effort that could be exerted on us by a stimulus or the effort that would be required to resist it; the activity scale has to do with the rapidity of movement expected of a stimulus-object—a temporal matter, whereas the potency scale is more connected with space.

Indeed, the three dimensions identified in Osgood's factor analyses are global, or as Heinz Werner would say, *syncretic*—merged together from several other distinct dimensions. Perhaps this is an artifact of the procedure of investigation and analysis, but perhaps also it reflects the syncretic character of some of our thinking. For example, size and weight are both measured by the potency dimension, perhaps reflecting the fact that it takes children a long time to realize that size is not necessarily correlated with weight—that big things, like balloons, can sometimes be quite the opposite of heavy.

A person's concepts can be regarded as being located in a "semantic space" of whatever number of dimensions are accepted as fundamental. (Although I have mentioned only three dimensions, there can be others.) The position of concepts in this semantic space can be averaged over individuals, to give

---

[12] C. E. Osgood. *Amer. Psychol.*, 1962, 17, 10–28.

results such as we have attempted to depict graphically in Figure 13. For some experimental purposes, it is useful to measure (1) the *polarity* of concepts, that is, their distance from the center or origin in the semantic space, and (2) the *distances* between concepts, that is, how different their "meanings" are.

It is unlikely, however, that the whole "meaning" of a concept can be indexed by the semantic differential technique, for the class of experiences represented by a concept cannot be completely described in the dimensional terms required by the technique. Note also that there is a certain artificiality in averaging results over many individuals. Concepts are essentially idiosyncratic, dependent on the individual's particular experiences, both verbal and nonverbal; any similarity between the concepts of different individuals

Figure 13. Locations of selected concepts in the semantic differential space defined by the three scales strong-weak, active-passive, *and* good-bad. *Concepts rated* good *are in lower-case letters, concepts rated* bad *are in capitals. (Data of J. J. Jenkins* et al. *An atlas of semantic profiles for 360 words.* Amer. J. Psychol., *1958, 71, 688–699.)*

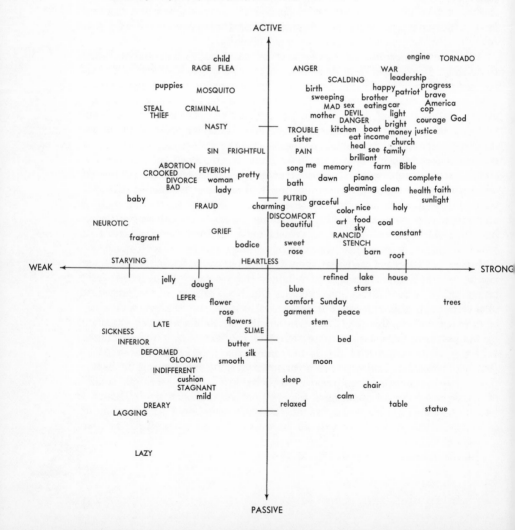

is a coincidence resulting from parallel experiences! One is tempted to call the semantic differential, instead, an "experiential" differential, since it indexes individuals' experiences or attitudes as classed into concepts. Groups of individuals are sometimes widely separated in their concepts; consider, for instance, how far apart pacifists and West Point graduates would be in their concept of *ARMY*.

Other Procedures
in the Study of Verbal Mediating Responses

The free association and semantic differential techniques are the only means devised thus far that are simple and convenient enough for cataloging the *properties* of concepts. But there are many techniques for studying the *role* of concepts and their associated mediation responses—various kinds of discrimination learning, concept formation, and verbal transfer experiments, some of which have already been described. These experiments clearly demonstrate that some kind of mediating process must intervene between the stimuli presented at the start of the experiment (the "initiating stimuli") and the final overt responses made by the subject (the "terminating" responses).

In Chapter 3 (pp. 35–36) we showed how meaning responses are established most probably by classical conditioning. This being the case, we can use the techniques of classical conditioning to investigate the relations between these meaning, or mediating, responses.

A reasonably convenient procedure is to condition a psychogalvanic reflex (PGR) to a word, X, by presenting the word several times together with a fairly loud buzzer sound. It is then possible to measure the degree to which the presentation of another word, Y, will elicit the same degree of PGR. This would be a measure, presumably, of the degree to which the mediated responses underlying the words have aspects in common. Bernard Riess[13] used this technique with children and found that at ages 8 and 11, homonyms produced a greater degree of generalization than synonyms, whereas this relation was reversed at ages 14 and 18½.

Arthur and Carolyn Staats have done much recent experimentation around the idea that even the noncriterial aspects of a concept, such as those measured by the semantic differential, can be conditioned. In one of their experiments,[14] subjects were told that they would later be asked to recall as many as possible of a series of nonsense syllables and meaningful words. The series contained six different nonsense syllables and 108 different words, but each of the six nonsense syllables was presented, at random points in the series, with a different one of 18 words. There was nothing special about the words paired with four of the nonsense syllables—words like *with, car, pen, four, this, sand*; but the words paired with *XEH*, for example, were words like *thief, bitter, ugly, sad, worthless, sour,* and those paired with *YOF* were words like *beauty, win, gift, sweet, honest,* and *smart*. After the series was presented, subjects were asked to rate the nonsense syllables on semantic differential scales. It was found that the syllables *XEH* and *YOF* were rated significantly dif-

---

13 B. F. Riess. *J. exp. Psychol.,* 1946, 36, 143–152.
14 C. K. Staats and A. W. Staats. *J. exp. Psychol.,* 1957, 54, 74–80.

ferently, and it could be inferred that a positive evaluative meaning had been conditioned to *YOF* and a negative one to *XEH*. Most of the subjects were unaware that there was any special relation between the nonsense syllables and the words, and results from those few who did become aware of the relation were not used. This experiment suggests that the meaning responses measured by the semantic differential can be conditioned to new stimuli. The experiment also shows, incidentally, how the conditioning of meaning responses plays a role in the development of a concept—for in this experiment subjects were forming concepts around the nonsense syllables *YOF* and *XEH*.

THE LINGUISTIC-RELATIVITY HYPOTHESIS

Now that we know something about the possible effects of language responses on thinking, we are in a better position to consider a formidable and persistent question that has been raised many times by philosophers and others interested in fundamental issues of human life. This question is the following: Does the structure and lexicon of the language we happen to speak affect our perceptions of the world and our dealings with it in any way that would be different if we happened to speak another language? This question has apparently arisen because languages obviously differ among themselves in many ways beyond the mere fact that different sounds are used to express the same meaning. The concepts symbolized by the forms, form-classes, and constructions of any one language do not always have exact counterparts in other languages; some would affirm that they *never* have exact counterparts in other languages. Anybody who has tried to make a really faithful translation from one language to another becomes painfully aware of these differences. If this is so, it would appear to follow that the thinking processes of the speakers of one language are not the same as the thinking processes of the speakers of any other language. Indeed, it would appear that a bilingual using one language thinks differently from the way he thinks in his other language.

The idea that the structure of one's language affects one's thought processes may be called the *linguistic-relativity hypothesis,* because it asserts that thought is relative to the language in which it is conducted. Sometimes, also, it is called the *linguistic Weltanschauung* hypothesis, because it is asserted that a particular language implies a unique "world-view" or perception of reality. A variant of this idea was suggested by German philosophers in the nineteenth century who claimed that Aristotle's logic would have been very different if he had been a Mexican. The most articulate modern spokesman for the theory of linguistic relativity was the linguist Benjamin Lee Whorf, and in one of the best statements of his point of view he wrote:

The background linguistic system (in other words, the grammar) of each language is not merely a reproducing instrument for voicing ideas but rather is itself the shaper of ideas, the program and guide for the individual's mental activity, for his analysis of impressions, for his synthesis of his mental stock in trade. Formulation of ideas is not an independent process, strictly rational in the old sense, but is part of a particular grammar and differs, from slightly to greatly, as between different grammars. We dissect nature along lines laid down by our native languages. The categories and types that we isolate from the world of phenomena we do not find there because they stare every observer in the face; on the contrary, the world is presented in a kaleidoscopic flux of impressions which has to be organized by our minds—and this means largely by the linguistic systems in our minds. We cut nature up, organize it into concepts, and ascribe significances as we do, largely because we are parties to an agreement to organize it in this way—an agreement that holds through our speech community and is codified in the patterns of our language. The agreement is, of course, an implicit and unstated one, BUT ITS TERMS ARE ABSOLUTELY OBLIGATORY; we cannot talk at all except by subscribing to the organization and classification of data which the agreement decrees.[15]

Before we can appraise the worth of the linguistic-relativity hypothesis, we should take a good look to see whether languages differ in their meaning structures as much as is claimed. Unfortunately, few systematic attempts have been made to compare languages in this respect, and it is a very difficult task in any case. It does little good to use a bilingual dictionary to find semantic and structural differences between languages, because it is the dictionary-maker's task, in this case, to identify *correspondences*, not differences, between the languages it deals with. Most of the differences between languages which have been cited in support of the linguistic-relativity hypothesis are striking, but possibly quite isolated cases, and it is always difficult to tell exactly what meanings are involved in each case. According to Whorf, in Shawnee, an Indian language, the expressions for "I push his head back" and "I dropped it in the water and it floated (bobbed back)" use the same basic verb form meaning "occurrence of a condition of force and reaction, pressure back, recoil" (see Figure 14). Whorf infers that the Shawnee perceives these two situations as highly similar, whereas the English speaker regards them as quite different. But how can we be sure? Are the English phrases given here adequate translations of the Shawnee expression? Finally, just because the Shawnees use the same verb form to refer to what are rather different physical actions, are we to infer that a similar mental process occurs in each case? We could doubtless find instances in English where a single verb form is used in highly different situations. For example, is *breaking* a fast in any real sense similar to *breaking* a stick? And are we perhaps not dealing with "dead metaphors"—as in the term *breakfast,* which would be rarely regarded by English speakers as a real breaking of a fast? When we cite differences between languages as evidence for differences in the mental processes of their speakers, we must realize that this is really no evidence at all; it merely points to the possibility of such differences in cognition that might be confirmed by appropriate investigation. That is, in order to establish that language differences correspond to differences in cognition, we must gather independent evidence about differences in cognition or other forms of nonlinguistic behavior.

In an earlier section we described the finding of Brown and Lenneberg that the ability of speakers of English to recognize and remember colors was related to the "codability" of those colors in English. Some colors were found to be highly codable—that is, subjects could name them promptly and with

[15] B. L. Whorf. *Language, thought, and reality.* (J. B. Carroll, ed.) Cambridge and New York: M.I.T.-Wiley, 1956, pp. 212–214.

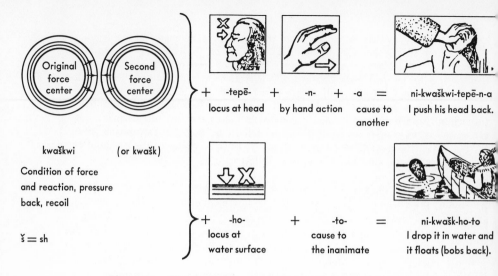

Figure 14. The English sentences I push his head back *and* I drop it in water and it floats *are unlike. But in Shawnee the corresponding statements are closely similar, emphasizing the fact that analysis of nature and classification of events as like or in the same category (logic) are governed by grammar. (From B. L. Whorf.* Language, thought, and reality *(J. B. Carroll, ed.). Cambridge-New York: M.I.T.-Wiley, 1956, p. 235.)*

high agreement; others were difficult to name. Lenneberg and an anthropologist, J. M. Roberts, investigated whether the same phenomenon would hold for speakers of the Zuni language, an American Indian language spoken in New Mexico. Striking differences between English and Zuni appeared; colors that were highly codable in English were not always highly codable in Zuni, and vice versa. And furthermore, Zuni speakers had more trouble in recognizing and remembering colors that were poorly coded in Zuni but well coded in English, and conversely for color ranges better coded in Zuni than in English. This experiment, published in 1956, was one of the first to give strong support to the linguistic-relativity hypothesis, although in the limited area of color perception.[16]

Another experiment done with American Indian languages suggests a further way in which language structure may influence behavior. Joseph Casagrande worked with groups of Navaho children living on the reservation. Some spoke only Navaho; others spoke only English, having been brought up in English-speaking Navaho families. Now, the Navaho language has the interesting characteristic that certain verbs of handling—the Navaho equivalents of *to pick up, to drop, to hold in the hand* and so on—require special forms depending on what kind of thing is being handled. There are eleven different forms, one for round spherical objects, one for round thin things, one for long flexible objects, and so forth, and the Navaho child has to learn

[16] E. H. Lenneberg and J. M. Roberts. *Indiana U. Pubs. in Anthrop. and Linguistics,* Memoir 13, 1956.

these in order to speak his language grammatically. Casagrande determined, first, that very young Navaho-speaking children did in fact know and use these forms correctly. He then compared the Navaho- and English-speaking children, matched for age, with respect to how often they used shape, form, or material as a basis for sorting objects, rather than color; he used sorting tasks that are usually performed by very young children on the basis of color. He found that Navaho-speaking children had a tendency to perform the sorting task on the basis of form at distinctly younger ages than the English-speaking children. Apparently, the fact that Navaho grammar requires the child to pay attention to the shapes, forms, and materials of things makes him more likely to guide his behavior on the basis of this aspect of his environment. Language, however, is not the only influence that can produce this result: Middle-class English-speaking children in metropolitan Boston performed the sorting task in about the same manner as the Navaho-speaking children, probably because of their abundant experience with shapes and forms in the toys they had played with.[17]

These experiments hardly touch upon "world-views" or philosophical orientations that might differentiate speakers of Zuni, Navaho, and English; there have been as yet no convincing demonstrations that languages impose different philosophical orientations. It is, in fact, difficult to find aspects of language structure that would suggest differences of this kind. What we do find is differences among languages with respect to the categories they require their speakers to pay attention to, and there is some promise that further research may confirm the relevance of these categories in directing behavior. For example, is it significant that in English, in contrast to the situation in many other languages, we are forced to indicate the sex of a person we refer to with a pronoun (*he, she*)? Does this mean that we are overanxious about whether the author of a scientific article is a man or a woman?

The question of whether the structure of a language can help or hinder problem-solving has not yet been definitively answered. If we could find cases in which one language has a code for a concept where another does not, we might expect that speakers of the first language would be more successful than speakers in the other, according to the experimental paradigm exemplified by Cofer's finding (p. 85) or the experiment of Spiker, Gerjuoy, and Shepard (page 94). Efforts to find such cases have been frustrated by the fact that apparently all languages have developed ways of coding the concepts required for the ordinary transactions in the environment that do not involve advanced science. For example, probably all languages, even those of primitive societies, have ways of saying "middle-sized," and in a concept-attainment task we would not expect adult speakers of various languages to differ, other things being equal, in their ability to attain the concept "middle-sized." ("Middle-sized" would not necessarily have to correspond with a single word.)

In fact, the similarities among languages seem to outweigh the differences. Even when free association and semantic differential techniques are used to

17 J. B. Carroll and J. B. Casagrande. In E. E. Maccoby *et al.* (Eds.). *Readings in social psychology* (3rd ed.). New York: Holt, Rinehart and Winston, 1958, pp. 18–31.

index differences between the concepts of speakers of different languages, the results are similar; differences can usually be interpreted as due to known cultural factors. Semantic differential research in a variety of cultures has shown that the same most salient factors show up: *evaluation, potency,* and *activity.* The positions of concepts in this semantic space are generally the same, and when they are not, explanations of the differences are usually readily at hand. For example, *rain* is a relatively unpleasant, depressing concept for speakers of English in an American college community, but it is quite "good" and "pleasant" for the Hopi Indians, for whom rainfall is scarce but essential.

To sum things up, the linguistic-relativity hypothesis has thus far received very little convincing support. Our best guess at present is that the effects of language structure will be found to be limited and localized.

This is not to deny that in learning a second language, a person will often be forced to channel his ways of expressing ideas differently. In Russian, "I had a book" is expressed as "to me was book." The English verb *to be* corresponds to either of two Spanish verbs, *ser* and *estar,* depending upon whether a state of affairs is conceived as relatively permanent, or temporary: "My father *is* a doctor" uses *ser,* while "The door *is* open" uses *estar.* Spanish thus makes a distinction which English does not ordinarily make. But the contrast of *temporary-permanent* is equally available to speakers of English and Spanish when it is truly critical.

LANGUAGE AND THOUGHT: A FINAL LOOK

From an early age, human beings develop internal processes that represent sensations and perceptions in such a way that they can be stored in memory and later brought into consciousness and manipulated in the absence of the stimuli that originally evoked them. Human beings can be aware of and respond to these internal processes, and when they learn language they are likely to call them by such terms as "thinking," "imagination," "imagery," "ideas," "concepts," "beliefs," and so on.

The child normally grows up in a social environment in which a particular language is in use among those who people that environment. This language exhibits a relationship to the internal processes of these language users in their own transactions with their environment.

In the early stage of language learning, the child's own preverbal internal processes are conditioned to the symbols used by others in his environment, but as the child assimilates the structure of his language, his internal processes become more and more like those of the speech community as a whole, at least insofar as these internal processes are represented in a language.

Thinking is the conscious or unconscious manipulation of internal processes for oneself, usually in some particular direction such as the solution of a problem. Communication, whether through language or through other means (such as music or painting), is behavior in which the initiator of the communication seeks (whether successfully or not) to arouse certain internal processes in the recipient of the communication and possibly to secure certain overt responses on his part.

Language symbols—or, rather, the internal processes that underlie given language symbols for the individual—may figure prominently in thinking and often determine its direction. The concepts named by language symbols—that is, verbal mediating processes—are "tools" of thought in these two senses: (1) They provide at least some of the internal stimuli and stimulus-producing responses that carry forward the sequences of events from the external stimuli initiating the process to the overt responses terminating it. And (2) they represent organizations of internal processes (acquired through learning or past experiences) that are potentially critical in determining whether a given sequence of thought will eventuate in successful or rewarded overt response. The possession of particular concepts acquired through past experience is a major factor in the solution of problems or the performance of tasks; indeed, the teaching of such concepts is one of the major functions of education. These concepts are usually, though not always, coded linguistically; some of the most important concepts for the solution of problems —concepts of identity, similarity, comparison of magnitudes, spatial position, temporal sequence, causation, and the like—are coded in the lexical and grammatical structure of a language. Nevertheless, many intellectual tasks can be performed without the use of linguistic codes.

Do specific language codes have an influence on the thinking processes? In principle, they can, if the above line of argumentation is accepted, and in certain instances they do. But it is unlikely that speakers of different languages have, by virtue of the languages they speak, different "world views," or different degrees of capacity to solve certain problems. There are more similarities than differences in the way language codes symbolize concepts, because these concepts are the result of the transactions of human societies with a physical and social environment that has many uniformities over the world. Even if there are differences, the basic intelligence of man is usually sufficient to overcome them.

Selected Readings

General, and Chapter 1

Brown, R. *Words and things.* Glencoe, Ill.: Free Press (Macmillan), 1958.

Carroll, J. B. *The study of language.* Cambridge: Harvard University Press, 1953.

Miller, G. A. *Language and communication.* New York: McGraw-Hill, 1951.

Saporta, S. (ed.). *Psycholinguistics: a book of readings.* New York: Holt, Rinehart, and Winston, 1961.

Chapter 2

Bloomfield, M. W., and L. Newmark. *A linguistic introduction to the history of English.* New York: Knopf, 1963.

Francis, W. N. *The structure of American English.* New York: Ronald, 1958.

Gleason, H. A., Jr. *An introduction to descriptive linguistics.* New York: Holt, Rinehart, and Winston, 1961. (*Revised edition.*)

Greenberg, J. H. (ed.). *Universals of language.* Cambridge: M.I.T. Press, 1963.

Ullmann, S. *Semantics: an introduction to the science of meaning.* New York: Barnes and Noble, 1962.

Chapter 3

Church, J. *Language and the discovery of reality.* New York: Random House, 1961.

Cofer, C. N., and B. S. Musgrave (eds.). *Verbal behavior and learning: problems and processes.* New York: McGraw-Hill, 1963.

Skinner, B. F. *Verbal behavior.* New York: Appleton-Century-Crofts, 1957.

Chapter 4

Garner, W. R. *Uncertainty and structure as psychological concepts.* New York: Wiley, 1962.

Miller, G. A., E. Galanter, and K. H. Pribram. *Plans and the structure of behavior.* New York: Holt, Rinehart, and Winston, 1960.

Mowrer, O. H. *Learning theory and the symbolic process.* New York: Wiley, 1960.

Penfield, W., and L. Roberts. *Speech and brain-mechanisms.* Princeton: Princeton University Press, 1959.

Chapter 5

Myklebust, H. R. *The psychology of deafness.* New York: Grune and Stratton, 1960.

Osgood, C. E., and M. S. Miron (eds.). *Approaches to the study of aphasia.* Urbana: University of Illinois Press, 1963.

Chapter 6

Bruner, J. S., J. J. Goodnow, and G. A. Austin. *A study of thinking.* New York: Wiley, 1956.

Humphrey, G. *Thinking: an introduction to its experimental psychology.* New York: Wiley, 1951.

Hunt, E. B. *Concept learning: an information processing problem.* New York: Wiley, 1962.

Hunt, J. McV. *Intelligence and experience.* New York: Ronald, 1961.

Chapter 7

Osgood, C. E., G. J. Suci, and P. H. Tannenbaum. *The measurement of meaning.* Urbana: University of Illinois Press, 1957.

Staats, A. W., and C. K. Staats. *Complex human behavior.* New York: Holt, Rinehart, and Winston, 1963.

Whorf, B. L. *Language, thought, and reality.* Cambridge: Technology Press, and New York: Wiley, 1956. (Edited by J. B. Carroll.)

Index

Comprehensibility, 60
Concept formation, unconscious, 82, 91
Concepts, 4, 5, 40, 41, 70, 73, 78, 80, 104, 106, 109, 111:
  attainment of, 81–84
  and form-classes, 92
  and language, 90–93
  and problem-solving, 84–86
Concrete operational thinking, 78–79
Conditioning:
  classical, 34–36, 39, 98, 105
  operant, 36, 39, 81, 98
Conjunctives, 92
Connotative meanings, 41, 88
Conservation of number, 79
Consonants, 11–12, 14, 17
Constructions, 10, 19–22, 27, 28, 50, 91
Content system, 6, 9, 26–29, 33
Context:
  and meaning, 26
  and redundancy, 56
Correlation, concept of, 92
Covert behavior, 76–78
Cramer, H. Leslie, 13
Criterial attributes, 40–41, 82, 101

D

Deaf, language learning of, 31, 73–74, 77
Declarative form, 51
Decoding, 71
Definitions, dictionary, 27
Delayed auditory feedback, 45
Deletion transformation, 25
Denotations, 26, 28
Dental consonants, 17
Determiner, 20
Determining tendency, 80
Dialect, 15
Dictionary, 27, 28, 107
Diphthong, 14
Discrimination:
  sounds, 59
  stimuli, 37–39
Distances, semantic, 104
Distinctive features, of phonemes, 17, 32
Double alternation problem, 93, 94
Drives, 80

E

Eaton, Helen, 91
Echoic responses, 36, 38
Edfeldt, Å. W., 77n
Education, and concept teaching, 111
Emphatic transformation, 21
Encoding, 71
English, 13, 19, 20, 21, 24, 62, 90, 108, 109
Environment, 72, 111:
  and individual differences, 69
Esperanto, 90
Euler circles, 87
Exclamations, 24
Exclamatory transformation, 21, 25
Existence-assertions, 24, 51, 60
Experience, classes of, 81, 91, 105
Expressions:
  constructionally ambiguous, 22
  nonsentential, 24

Expression system, 6, 9, 29, 33, 40, 51
Expression-types, 24–25, 29, 51
Expressive movements, 3

F

Factor analysis, 67, 102
Factors of language ability, 67–68
Feedback, 45, 77
Festinger, Leon, 80
Finnish, 62
Flanagan, B., 72n
Fletcher, Harvey, 12
Fluency of expression, 68
Foreign language aptitude tests, 66, 68
Foreign languages, learning of, 42
Form, 10, 13, 18–19, 22, 27, 34, 91
Formal propositional thinking, 78, 79
Formants, 12
Form classes, 20, 28, 33, 48, 50, 61:
  learning of, 33
Formulation, verbal, 82
Frequency of language units, 52–54, 63, 100
Freud, Sigmund, 71
Fricative consonants, 17
Friedman, Elizabeth A., 53
Fries, Charles C., 23–24
Functional fixedness, 85
Functions of language, 4
Function words, 27
Furth, Hans, 73

G

Garner, Wendell R., 55n
Gelfand, Sidney, 85
Gerjuoy, Irma R., 94, 109
Gestures, 3
Goldiamond, Israel, 72n, 76n
Goldman-Eisler, Frieda, 47
Goldstein, Kurt, 70
Goodnow, Jacqueline, 83
Grammar, 9, 19–21, 23, 27, 29, 52:
  learning of, 32
Grammatical "depth," 52
Grammatical sensitivity, 68
Grapheme, 62–63
Greenberg, Joseph, 29n
Greetings, 24
Griffith, Belver C., 59n

H

Hall, Edward T., 3, 43
Harris, Katherine S., 59n
Hawkins, William F., 76n
Hayakawa, S. I., 96
Heidbreder, Edna, 83
Heise, George A., 56, 57
Henle, Mary, 86
Heredity, 30–31, 69, 72
Herman, David T., 97n
Hesitation phenomena, 47
Hoffman, Howard S., 59n
Hogan, H. P., 96
Hopi Indians, 110
Hovland, Carl I., 95
Howes, Davis, 49, 54, 64, 71, 100

Hypotheses, in concept-formation experiments, 84

I

Ideas, 34
Ideational fluency, 67
Imperative form, 51
Imperative transformation, 21, 25, 61
Individual differences, 47, 65
Informant, 22
Information, 4:
    bit of, 55
    theory, 54–58
Inner speech, 76, 77
Instruction, verbal, 94
Intelligence, 111:
    tests, 66
Intelligibility, of speech, 58–59
Intention, 42
International Phonetic Alphabet, 10, 15
Interpretation, 42
Interrogative transformation, 21, 25, 61
Intonation, 16, 29, 34
Intransitive verb, 24
Introspection, 2, 34
Invariants, 40
Italian, 28

J

Jakobson, Roman, 32
James, William, 82
Japanese, 62
Jenkins, James J., 48n, 71, 99n, 104
Judson, Abe J., 85
Juncture, 15, 16, 29

K

Kees, Weldon, 3
Keller, Helen, 40n
Kent-Rosanoff list, 48, 99n
Kernel sentence, 25, 50
Kjeldergaard, Paul M., 49n
Kurtz, Kenneth H., 95

L

Labels, verbal, 96, 97
Labiodental consonants, 17
Language:
    in animals, 30
    and cognition, 89–111
    definition, 3
    functions of, 4
    learning of, 23, 30–43
    primitive, 10
    as sign system, 8–28
    silent, 3
    statistical structure of, 52–58
    written, 47
Language units, frequency of, 52–54, 63, 100
Latin, 19, 28
Lawless, R. H., 97n
Learning:
    discrimination, 31
    formal, informal, and technical, 43
    of language, 23, 30–42, 110
    of second language, 42–43
Leeper, Robert, 82n

Lenneberg, Eric H., 95, 107, 108
Lexicography, 27
Liberman, Alvin M., 59n
Lichten, W., 56, 57
Linguistic relativity, hypothesis of, 106–110
Linguistics, descriptive, 8–9:
    methodology, 22–26, 29
Linguistic units, 18, 24, 27, 59
Linking verb, 24, 51
Lipreading, 74
Logic and thinking, 86–88
Lorge, Irving, 53

M

Maier, Norman, 85, 86
Mand (response), 37–38
Marshall, R. W., 97n
Meaning, 6, 9, 16, 24, 78, 88, 91, 102:
    analysis of content system, 26–28
    connotative, 41
    denotative, 40–41
    as psychological problem, 33–42
    situational, 41 -42
Meaningfulness, 41, 100
Mediating processes, 36, 40, 97–106, 111
Mednick, Sarnoff A., 35n, 36n, 38n, 83n
Memory:
    aided by verbal learning, 95
    storage capacity of, 52
Mental retardation, 69–70
Methodology, of linguistics, 22–26, 29
Miller, George A., 50, 52, 53, 56–58
Miller, Neal, 34
Minimal pairs, 14–15, 59
Miron, Murray S., 7n
Mitford, Jessica, 88
Morpheme, 19, 26, 27, 32, 60
Morphology, 19, 22, 29
Motivation, of speech, 46, 71
Mowrer, O. Hobart, 61

N

Names, 94
Naming facility, 68
Naming stage, 32
Nasal consonants, 17
Natural languages, 3, 90
Navaho language, 108, 109
Negative transformation, 21, 25
Neurosis, effect on language, 71
Newman, Edwin B., 53
Noble, Clyde E., 41
Noise, 59
Nominals, 24, 92
Nonsentential expressions, 51
Norcross, Kathryn, 97
Noun, 9, 20:
    count, 33
    mass, 33
Null-transformation, 25, 61
Number system, 4

O

Object, of transitive verb, 24
Ogden, C. K., 91
Oléron, Pierre, 73
Operant response, 36, 76 (*see also* Conditioning):
    paradigms, 37

Oral speech ability, 68
Orders of approximation, 56–58
Orienting reflex, 80
Orthographies, 62
Oscilloscope, 12
Osgood, Charles E., 49, 70–71, 102–103
Osler, Sonia F., 98*n*
Overt response, 35

P

Paradigmatic responses, 48
Paradigms, for learning of language, 34, 37
Paranomia, 71
Passive transformation, 21, 25
Pattern playback device, 12
Penfield, Wilder, 45–46
Perception, 70:
 of printed words, 63, 76
 of reality, 106
 of sounds, 12
Perceptual invariants, 40, 78, 80
Perceptual response, 35, 39
Persuasive language, 88
Philosophy, and study of meaning, 33
Phoneme-grapheme correspondences, 68
Phonemes, 6, 10, 12–17, 19, 22, 29, 59, 74:
 learning of, 32
 segmental, 14, 16, 60, 62
 suprasegmental, 15, 16, 62
Phonemics, 11
Phonemic symbols, 15
Phonetics, 10, 11
Phonics, 63
Phrase:
 noun, 20
 verb, 20
Phrase-structures, 23
Piaget, Jean, 78, 79
Pitch phonemes, 14–16
Polarity, of concepts, 104
Predicate, of sentence, 20, 24
Predication, 24, 50–51, 61
Preoperational stage of thinking, 78
Prepositionals, 92
Prepositions, 27
Printed words, perception of, 63
Problem-solving, 80, 84–86, 109
Processes, 22
Production, of speech, 73
Programed instruction, 83
Pronoun, 20
Psychogalvanic response (PGR), 34, 105
Psychology, and linguistics, 9, 28–29
Psychosis, effect on language, 71

R

Rank-frequency relationship, 53–54
Rate:
 of reading, 64–65
 of talking, 2, 46, 60
 of writing, 2
Readability, 64
Reading, 61–65:
 readiness tests, 67
 silent, 77
Reasoning, 93:
 ability, 67
 faulty, 87–88

Recognition, 76
Redundancy, 56, 59, 60
Referents, 33:
 referential meaning, 6
Réflexion parlée, 93
Reinforcement, 16, 36, 38, 43, 46
Response:
 echoic, 36, 38
 mediating, 36, 40
 texting, 38
Responses:
 overt, 35
 paradigmatic and syntagmatic, in free
  association, 48
 perceptual, 35, 39
Response sentences, 23, 25
Reversible thinking, 79
Rewrite rule, 20, 21, 23, 29, 52
Riess, Bernard, 105
Roberts, J. M., 108
Roberts, Lamar, 46
Ruesch, Jurgen, 3
Russell, Wallace A., 48*n*, 99*n*, 101
Russian, 110

S

Saccadic eye movements, 63
Sayers, B. M., 73
Schizophrenia, 71
Scholastic Aptitude Test, 68
Schuell, Hilda, 71
Second language learning, 42, 110
Semantic differential, 88, 102–105, 109–
 110
Semantic fallacies, 96
Semantics (*see* Meaning)
Semantic space, 103, 104, 110
Semivowels, 14, 17
Sentence, 20, 21, 41:
 "depth" of grammar, 52
 as discriminative stimuli, 61
 situation, sequence, and response sen-
  tences, 23
Sentence completion tests, 66
Sentence types, 24, 51, 60
Sequence sentences, 23, 25
Set, 49, 80, 99
Shadowing technique, 73
Shannon, Claude, 54
Shawnee, 107, 108
Shepard, Winifred O., 94, 95, 109
Signs, 33
Sign system, 5–7, 9
Silent language, 3
Situation sentences, 23
Size of vocabulary, 27
Skinner, B. F., 36, 38, 39
Slips of the tongue, 71
Sound spectrograph, 12, 13
Sounds:
 discrimination of, 59
 of language, 10–12
 perception, 12
Space, semantic, 103, 104, 110
Spanish, 62, 110
Specific language disability, 69
Spectator behavior, 84
Spectrograph, sound, 12, 13